Warman's®

U.S. Coins & Currency

FIELD GUIDE

3rd Edition

✓ W9-BFV-573

Arlyn G. Sieber

Values and Identification

Published by

krause publications
A subsidiary of F+W Media, Inc.

700 East State Street • Iola, WI 54990-0001
715-445-2214 • 888-457-2873
www.krausebooks.com

Our toll-free number to place an order or obtain
a free catalog is (800) 258-0929.

Library of Congress Control Number: 2009923224

ISBN-13: 978-1-4402-0365-7
ISBN-10: 1-4402-0365-2

Designed by Rachael Knier
Edited by Justin Moen

Printed in China

ACKNOWLEDGMENTS

Special thanks to the following
for providing the spectacular color
photography that made this book possible:

COINS

Heritage Numismatic Auctions, Inc.
3500 Maple Ave., 17th Floor
Dallas, TX 75219-3941
214-528-3500
800-US COINS (872-6467)
http://coins.ha.com

PAPER MONEY

Chester L. Krause

2006-2008 State Quarter,
2007-2008 Presidential Dollar,
2007-2008 First Spouse Gold $10,
and 2009 Lincoln Cent reverse images
from the United States Mint

CONTENTS

INTRODUCTION

"Warman's U.S. Coins & Currency Field Guide, 3rd Edition" provides a quick overview of the hobby and a general feel for the background, characteristics, and values of each of the common categories presented in an easily portable format. Because this book is only an introduction to the subject, only brief information is given on early coins and paper money. Photos and listings focus on items from the early 1800s and later, which are the items most likely to be encountered today.

1894 Morgan Dollar

WHY COLLECT?

There are as many different ways to collect coins and paper money as there are individual, creative collectors. But most of these collectors are motivated by one or more of several common goals:

Fun: Many collectors are excited by the "thrill of the hunt." They enjoy the challenge of chasing down the date or mint-mark they need to complete a series, or even part of one. Many people call just the first or last part of a series a "short set," and its completion can be a satisfying milestone on the road to completing a more difficult series.

History: Many history buffs collect coins. Coins are among the most commonly available artifacts of the past. Unlike stamps, which were not introduced until the 1840s, coins and paper money of some sort from the early days of colonial settlement in North America are available. Just think of owning a Carson City silver dollar from the Old West or a pine tree shilling once spent by one of the original Pilgrims.

Art: Coins and paper money are great ways to learn about artistic trends and are much more affordable than many other forms of art. Many admire the quality of engraving by such masters as Augustus Saint-Gaudens or James Earle Fraser. Since the 1980s, even modern art has had its place on American commemoratives.

Relaxation: Any absorbing hobby can provide hours of relaxation. Everyone can appreciate a few hours of quiet diversion, an escape from the mundane cares of the world.

Investment: Some collect primarily as an investment, expecting that the coins they buy will increase in value over the years. Not all coins increase in value, especially inexpensive ones. It is a challenge to predict the ones that will. Still, many have profited from collectible coins, especially if the coins are popular and correctly graded. Investment may also be a secondary motive for those who collect for other reasons. The decision to buy a Morgan dollar may be based on fun; the decision to buy one in a particular grade may be based on its investment potential.

WHAT TO COLLECT

With all the different approaches to collecting, most collectors in North America started their hobby the same way: by assembling a series of coins from pocket change. Longtime collectors still check the Lincoln cents in their change, hoping to find a date needed to fill a hole in a folder. The lowly Lincoln cent still gives them a sense of where they have been in their collecting journey and how they got there. The U.S. Mint's 50 State Quarters program has also renewed interest in collecting coins from circulation.

Of course it doesn't take long before collectors ask what other coins and paper money are available besides those in their pockets. There are not only the older issues, long hoarded out of circulation, but also new special issues, struck sparingly and sold by the Mint at a premium to collectors. Despite the natural incli-

The 50 State Quarters program provided a new opportunity to collect coins from circulation.

nation to specialize right away, it is probably wise not to do so too soon. Exploring many different types of coins and paper money can lead to exciting fields you may not discover if you decide to confine your interests too soon. Eventually most collectors do specialize, but it's good to explore first the wide range of available material. This field guide can help in that process.

Collectors whose primary interest is history often choose to focus on a particular era or country. They might seek one coin from each king of England or France, or as many different types of paper money as one can from a particular era as they can afford. On the other hand, if you are a fan of technology, understanding how coins are made may interest you. You may hopscotch across the centuries to see how technology evolved from hammering to roller dies to screw presses to electric power. Studying error coins is one of the best ways to understand how coins are made, and error-coin collectors are less often deceived by counterfeits because of that knowledge.

Collectors who focus on art will, of course, follow their own tastes. Many who favor classic styles seek the coins of ancient Greece or the U.S. silver and gold issues introduced during President Theodore Roosevelt's administration. Those who like progressive trends in modern art will certainly find 20th-century European coinage interesting. Some collectors focus on what is depicted rather than the style. For example, many collectors focus on collecting coins and paper money depicting favorite animals or ships.

Coin shows big and small bring together collectors and dealers.

Coin collecting can be inexpensive; it can also be costly, depending on your goals. Set your sight on coins that you can afford. If you can afford only one coin of a particular series a year, the waiting will soon take the enthusiasm out of your hunt. There are plenty of interesting coins out there for under a dollar. Also, if you aren't investing, don't feel the need to pour your money into the highest quality coins. If a good middle grade coin pleases you, then don't push your financial limits.

HOW TO LEARN MORE

Join a coin club. Not only is social contact one of the most enjoyable aspects of the hobby, the knowledge and guidance you will get from fellow collectors is invaluable. Another source of guidance is a dependable dealer. Not all dealers are tried and true, but most take care of "their" collectors—the hobbyists they see regularly and with whom they seek to forge a long-term relationship. Even if you are not buying coins or bank notes on each visit to the shop, stop in whenever you're in the area to pick up a numismatic magazine or book, or just to ask what's new in the dealer's inventory. It will show the dealer that you take the hobby seriously and that it will be worth their efforts to take the time to work with you. Grading is especially difficult to learn without the aid of an honest dealer willing to let you examine more coins than you will ever have need to own.

STATE OF THE MARKET

The worst U.S. economic crises since the Great Depression has made for uncertainty in every sector of the nation's economy, including the market for collectible coins. For the most part, however, numismatic collectibles held their own against these challenges, particularly scarce and rare issues among traditional material.

Precious-metals prices form the base values for any coins containing one of the metals, such as gold and silver. In 2008, gold averaged almost $890 a troy ounce in January and then flirted with the $1,000 level in March. It ended up averaging $968 a troy ounce for the month. It dropped to about $890 a troy ounce on average again in June before spiking to an average of almost $940 a troy ounce in July.

As U.S. and other world financial markets worsened in late 2008, gold dropped too. It averaged $839 a troy ounce in August, $830 in September, $806 in October, and $760 in November. It rallied a bit at year's end to average $816 a troy ounce in December. It closed the year at almost $870 a troy ounce. It was trading for about $950 a troy ounce in mid 2009.

Like gold, silver spiked in early 2008. It ended March 6, 2008, at $20.80 a troy ounce. But also like gold, the bottom fell out of price levels later in the year. Silver ended 2008 at $10.79 a troy ounce but held close to that level in early 2009 trading.

Through all the gut-wrenching economic woes of 2008, demand in the coin market maintained a remarkable level. "Even with tight money, major rarities are strong," said Harry Miller, market analyst for *Numismatic News*. "There is continued, broadly based demand in anything scarce."

Modern collector material—recently issued commemoratives, proof sets, mint sets, and other U.S. Mint products—have not performed as well as their more traditional scarce and rare counterparts. The U.S. Mint saw its inventories of current offerings not moving as expected and announced steps in late 2008 to reduce those stockpiles and keep them at manageable levels in the future.

The year 2008 marked the completion of the 10-year 50 State Quarters program. Six more circulating quarters, however, were scheduled for release in 2009 to honor the District of Columbia and five U.S. territories: the Commonwealth of Puerto Rico, Guam, American Samoa, the U.S. Virgin Islands, and the Commonwealth of the Northern Mariana Islands. The obverse for each coin will be the traditional portrait of George Washington.

The Presidential $1 coin series was also scheduled to continue in 2009 with releases honoring William Henry Harrison, John Tyler, James K. Polk, and Zachary Taylor. The First Spouse Gold Coins series began in 2007 and honors the nation's first spouses on half-ounce gold $10 coins (0.9999 fine). Scheduled for release in 2009 were issues honoring Anna Harrison, Letitia Tyler, Julia Tyler, Sarah Polk, and Margaret Taylor.

The reverse of the circulating Sacagawea dollar coin was scheduled to change in 2009 to begin a series honoring Native Americans. The reverse design selected for the first issue features a Native American woman planting seeds in a field of corn, beans and squash. Also scheduled to make their debut in 2009 were a series of circulating Lincoln cents commemorating the bicentennial of Abraham Lincoln's birth and the centennial of the Lincoln cent. The traditional obverse introduced in 1909, featuring a bust of Lincoln, will continue, but four new reverses will be issued in approximately three-month intervals.

Also scheduled for release in 2009 were silver dollars commemorating Lincoln and the bicentennial of Louis Braille's birth. A 2009 version of Augustus Saint-Gaudens classic ultra-high-relief gold $20 coin, or double eagle, may make the biggest market splash of all new or recent U.S. Mint collector products.

VALUES

Coin and paper money prices can be as volatile as the stock market. Although some coins and notes remain stable for years, others skyrocket during a period of popularity and then plummet when they fall out of fashion. The listings presented here are guides to retail values—the approximate prices collectors can expect to pay when purchasing coins from a dealer—at the time of publication. Because the law of supply and demand ultimately rules, the final decision about a coin's value lies with the buyer and seller.

Dealers are in business to make a living. This means they must pay less than the retail values listed in this field guide when they buy coins. Depending on the value and demand, a dealer will pay from 10 to 90 percent of the retail value of coins or paper money listed here.

In most cases, the grades listed represent the conditions and corresponding values collectors will most likely encounter for a particular series in the market. Some recent coins are priced in grades MS-63 or MS-65 because typical uncirculated (MS-60) coins, even when first released, normally do not merit a value significantly above face value.

SIZES

Coins and paper money are not shown to scale in this field guide. Most coins have been enlarged to show more detail, all paper money has been reduced to fit the pages. Thus, do not rely on the size of the photos for identification. Instead, focus on the information stamped or printed on the coins or bills, and the captions and listings accompanying them.

COIN INTRODUCTION
INTRODUCTION TO U.S. COINS

A typical 18th-century American living in the 13 Colonies would not have found many English silver or gold coins in his pocket. It was British policy to restrict the export of precious metals to the Colonies. As a result, only copper was struck for the Colonies, and even that was rarely minted.

Silver coins were so scarce that Colonial Americans used any foreign silver or gold coins that could be pressed into service. Besides Spanish coins, French, Portuguese, and occasionally German silver and gold were readily accepted when they turned up.

French Colonies 1762A Sou Marque

Some of the Colonial governors also issued paper money valued in terms of discounted British currency, or in Spanish milled dollars. After the Declaration of Independence, many of the same forms of currency continued. Spanish colonial silver and gold were as popular as ever. All the new states issued their own paper money.

Some states issued their own official coinage, too, when the Articles of Confederation governed the country. When the Constitution took effect in 1789, it ended state-issued coinage. The new, stronger federal union led many to promote a national coinage. Others argued that it was not the place of government to get involved in such things. Supported by President George Washington, proponents of a national mint prevailed, and construction began in 1792.

1792 silver five-cent piece, also known as a "half disme."

For administrative and technical reasons, the new U.S. Mint got off to a slow start, but before the end of 1792, about 25,000 silver five-cent pieces, known as "half dismes," were struck. The new coinage was based on a decimal system dividing a dollar into 100 cents. The idea of the dollar as the standard unit was inspired by the Spanish piece of eight, then common in the Colonies.

The new Mint struggled to meet the nation's coinage needs as it fought shortages of bullion and labor, and annual yellow-fever epidemics. Many of the silver and gold coins it did produce were withdrawn from circulation and melted by speculators because the coins were undervalued relative to their precious-metal content. The endeavor became so futile that the striking of many denominations was frequently suspended. It wasn't until the 1830s that coin weights were adjusted to prevent their export.

During the Mint's first four decades, every die was engraved by hand, so no two were exactly alike. Also, the coins were struck by hand on a screw press one at a time. Finally, in 1836, the Industrial Revolution came to the U.S. Mint. Steam-powered equipment was imported from England. Almost overnight American coins became more uniform, and the old lettered edges were replaced by modern reeding.

Also, the quantities that could be produced increased dramatically. This technological improvement roughly coincided with a needed reduction in the coins' bullion content and with a facelift for all silver denominations. Thus, during the mid-

1830s, the nation's coinage was transformed. The silver three-cent piece and three new gold denominations—$3 (1854) and $1 and $20 (1849)—were introduced, partially because of the California Gold Rush.

But the big event of the mid-century was the coinage law of 1857. This law eliminated the half cent, reduced the size of the cent from bigger than a quarter to the diameter used today, and, most important, no longer allowed foreign silver and gold to be legal tender in the United States. All the changes finally allowed the Mint to provide a true national coinage.

Civil War coin shortages resulted in many privately issued tokens and also inspired the two-cent and nickel three-cent pieces. They may also have played a role in the introduction of the nickel five-cent in 1866. It also saw the debut of the motto

1873 Silver Three-Cent Piece

1860S Gold Three-Dollar Piece

"In God We Trust" on U.S. coins. During the late 1860s and 1870s, the nation was in the economic doldrums. Mintages were low for many denominations, particularly the silver dollar, and hence many coins from those years are scarce today.

From the late 1870s onward, coinage was plentiful for half a century—sometimes too plentiful. A dominant political influence of the time was the Free Silver Movement, which advocated the striking of unlimited quantities of silver coins to use up the large amount of the precious metal that was being mined. This, in turn, would increase the money supply, which would cause inflation to erode debts.

From 1873 to 1918 and later, several laws were passed that forced the government to buy silver and strike an abundance of silver dollars. Unpopular in the more developed parts of the country, many of the dollar coins sat in government or bank vaults for decades. Minor silver also became more common during this era.

Early in the 20th century, Theodore Roosevelt led the nation to a new level of intellectual consciousness, promoting ideas as diverse as national parks and the artistic merits of the nation's coinage. For the latter, he looked outside the Mint and sought the greatest sculptors of the day. Most of the new coin designs reflected neo-classical artistic trends also prevalent in Europe. The beautiful designs include the so-called Mercury dime, the Walking Liberty half dollar, and the Saint-Gaudens gold $20, as well as the less classically inspired Buffalo nickel.

The first U.S. commemorative coins were also struck in 1892, providing an outlet for artists of various influences. But by 1936, the program had gotten out of hand with a proliferation of coins commemorating local themes rather than themes

1892 Commemorative Columbian Half Dollar

of national interest. In that one year alone, 22 different half dollars were struck.

The need for strategic metals for armaments during World War II led to temporary changes in U.S. coins. Cents dated 1943 were struck in zinc-coated steel, and nickels dated 1943-1945 were struck in a copper-silver-manganese alloy.

Idealistic images of Liberty were gradually replaced during the 1930s and 1940s with those of statesmen, and designs were opened to competitions.

An increase in the price of silver in 1964 prompted massive hoarding of silver coins as the value of their precious-metal content approached their face values. As a result, silver was partially or completely removed from coinage in favor of a base-metal clad composition, which can be readily distinguished by the copper core visible on the edge. The cent, too, was debased in 1982. The bronze alloy was replaced by copper-plated zinc.

Commemorative coins also resumed in 1982. Abuses similar to those of the 1930s befell the program in the 1990s, but laws

1943S Zinc-Coated Steel Lincoln Cent

limiting the number of programs in a year have since been passed. Congress has also mandated collectible circulating-coin programs, such as the successful 50 State Quarters program and the Westward Journey Nickel Series of 2004-2006.

COIN MINTS AND MINTMARKS

The first U.S. mint was constructed in Philadelphia in 1792. The city continues to be home to what is considered the main U.S. mint. Production facilities in other cities are considered branch mints, but this does not mean that the largest quantities of each coin are always struck in Philadelphia.

The first branch mints were established in the South to bring coin production closer to newly found deposits of precious metals. Mints in Charlotte, N.C., Dahlonega, Ga.,

2008W Silver One-Ounce American Eagle

and New Orleans produced coins from 1838 through 1861. Charlotte and Dahlonega produced only gold coins; New Orleans produced gold and silver coins. New Orleans also produced coins from 1879 through 1909.

The San Francisco Mint opened in 1854 to process bullion from the California Gold Rush. Today, it strikes most U.S. proof coins. In 1870, the silver mining boom in Nevada prompted the opening of the Carson City Mint in that state. It closed in 1893, and its coins are generally scarce.

The Denver facility officially became a branch mint in 1906 after originally operating as an assay office since 1863. Its production numbers have rivaled Philadelphia's in some years.

The West Point Mint in West Point, N.Y., is not as well known as a coin-production facility as its more traditional counterparts in Philadelphia, Denver and San Francisco. It was built in 1937 as the West Point Bullion Depository, an adjunct of the New York Assay Office.

It produced one-cent coins without a mintmark from 1973 to 1986 as an adjunct of the Philadelphia Mint. It was officially designated a U.S. branch mint in 1988 and continues to produce commemorative coins and American Eagle bullion coins.

Mintmarks—in the form of a small letter on U.S. coins—indicate which mint struck a coin. The following mintmarks appear on U.S. coins. Issues without mintmarks were struck at Philadelphia or, as noted above, West Point.

P	Philadelphia	**D**	Denver
C	Charlotte, N.C.	**O**	New Orleans
CC	Carson City, Nev.	**S**	San Francisco
D	Dahlonega, Ga.	**W**	West Point, N.Y.

COIN GRADING

A coin's value is determined in part by its grade, or state of preservation. Grading terms provide a concise method for describing a coin's condition, particularly when a dealer or collector advertises a coin for sale in a magazine. Several grading-guide books, which illustrate and describe U.S. coins in different series in different grades, are commonly used by dealers and collectors. Among them is *The Official American Numismatic Association Grading Standards for United States Coins.*

Following are commonly used grading terms and a general description of each:

Uncirculated (Unc.), or **mint-state (MS)**, coins have no wear on them. Mint-state coins are further graded on a numerical scale from 60 to 70, with MS-70 being theoretical perfection. Although mint-state coins may show no wear from circulation, they can still vary in condition. For example, after coins are struck, they are loaded into bags and then shipped from the mint. Scuff marks occur when the coins bang into

*The Professional Coin Grading
Service was the first grading
service to encapsulate
coins after grading.*

each other while being shipped in the bags. Although the coins may not show wear from circulation, these "bag marks" can detract from their condition.

Some professional grading services use all 11 increments from 60 to 70 in grading mint-state coins. Some traditionalists, however, believe it's impossible to tell a one-point difference in mint-state grades. The ANA grading guide, for example, lists and describes only MS-60, MS-63, MS-65, and MS-67.

Brilliant uncirculated (BU) refers to a mint-state coin retaining all or most of its original luster. It may have a numeric grade of MS-60 to MS-70. In the case of higher grades, many dealers prefer to use the more precise numeric grades.

MS-67

MS-67 is the nearest thing to a perfect coin that is likely to appear on the market. It may have the faintest of bag marks discernible only through a magnifying glass. Copper must have luster.

MS-65

MS-65 describes an exceptional coin and is most commonly the highest grade used when grading conservatively. It will have no significant bag marks, particularly in open areas such as the field or the cheek of a person portrayed on the coin. Copper may have toning. Fewer than one coin in hundreds qualifies for this grade. MS-65 coins are among the most popular sought by investors.

MS-63

MS-63 coins are pleasant, collectible examples that exhibit enough bag marks to be noticed but not so many that the coins are considered marred, with particularly few on open areas, such as the fields or a cheek.

MS-60

MS-60 describes coins that saw considerable scuffing at the mint before their release. They will often have nicks and discoloration. Sometimes called "commercial uncirculated," they may actually be less pleasant to behold than a higher-grade circulated coin.

AU

About uncirculated (AU) describes coins with such slight signs of wear that a mild magnifying glass may be needed to see them. A trace of luster should be visible. One should be careful not to confuse an attractive AU coin for uncirculated.

EF

Extremely fine (EF, XF) is the highest grade for a coin that exhibits wear significant enough to be seen easily by the unaided eye. The coin still exhibits extremely clear minute detail. In the case of U.S. coins with the word "Liberty" on a headband or shield, all letters must be sharp and clear. Many XF coins exhibit luster, but it is not necessary for the grade.

VF

Very fine (VF) coins show obvious signs of wear. Nevertheless, most of the design detail is still clear, making for an overall pleasant coin. On American coins with "Liberty" on a headband or shield, all letters must be clear.

Fine (F) is the lowest grade most people consider collectible. About half the design details show for most types. On U.S. coins with "Liberty," all letters must be visible if not sharp.

VG

Very good (VG) coins exhibit heavy wear. All outlines are clear, as is generally the rim. Some internal detail also shows, but most is worn off. At least three letters of "Liberty" must be legible; all letters must be present on pre-1857 copper coins and Morgan silver dollars.

Good (G) coins are generally considered uncollectible except for novelty purposes. The design usually shows no internal detail. Some of the rim may also be worn off. "Liberty" is worn off on most coins and shows just trace elements on pre-1857 copper coins and Morgan silver dollars.

About good (AG) and **fair (FR)** are grades in which only scarce coins are collected. Many collectors would rather do without the coin than to add an AG example to their collections. The rim will be worn down, and some outline of the design may be gone.

Poor (PR) is the lowest possible grade. Many coins in grade poor will not even be identifiable. When identifiable, many will still be condemned to the melting pot. Few collectors would consider owning such a coin unless it's an extreme rarity.

"Proof" denotes a special way of making coins for presentation or sale by the Mint directly to collectors. A proof coin is usually double struck with highly polished dies on polished blanks, yielding a mirrorlike finish.

In the past, matte, or sandblasted, proofs were popular. They were characterized by a non-reflective but highly detailed surface. "Cameo proofs" are struck with dies polished only in the fields. The design details, such as the portrait, have a dull finish for a cameo effect. Some cameo proofs command premium values over regular proofs.

Under the ANA grading system, proof grades use the same numbers as circulated and uncirculated grades, and the amount of wear on the coin corresponds to those grades. But the number is preceded by the word "proof"—proof-65, proof-55, proof-45, and so on. The ANA says a proof coin with

Proof

many marks, scratches, or other defects should be called an "impaired proof."

Other miscellaneous factors can affect a coin's quality. The presence of all or part of the original luster usually increases a coin's value. Be careful, however, not to be fooled by a coin that has been dipped in a brightener to simulate this luster artificially.

Toning, or a natural coloration on a coin obtained over time, can be good or bad. If the toning is dull, irregular, or splotchy, it is likely to be considered unpleasant, and many collectors may choose to avoid it even if it is a high-grade coin.

On the other hand, if the toning is mild or displays a "halo effect" around a coin's edge, or is composed of pleasant iridescent shades, many collectors and dealers would pay a premium to obtain it based on its "eye appeal." Standard phrases used

Poor Toning

Ideal Toning

to denote a coin's eye appeal when grading include "premium quality" (PQ) and "prooflike" (PL).

Also, mints sometimes strike coins on blanks with minor imperfections. Poor mixing of the metals in the alloy or flaws left by trapped gas from this same process are examples. If trivial, they may be ignored on most coins, but on more expensive or high-grade pieces, concern over these flaws may increase.

Even on circulated coins, few collectors want examples with scratches or edge nicks. These will occur even more frequently on larger coins, such as silver dollars, or coins with reeded edges. Depending on extent, such coins may be discounted a little or a lot.

Of course, coins with damage are worth far less than coins without. Many coins have been mounted for use in jewelry, and even when the loop or bezel has been removed, they may still show slight signs of this unfortunate experience. A few collectors consider these situations opportunities to acquire coins with high-grade detail for a fraction of the cost. It should be remembered that the same heavy discount will apply when the collector resells the coins.

HANDLING AND TREATMENT OF COINS

How a collector or dealer treats their coins can greatly affect how well they hold their value. Metal is more reactive and

If one must handle a coin, it should only be touched by the edge.
Never touch a coin's obverse or reverse surface.

softer than many people think. In some cases, simply touching a coin can contribute to its deterioration. This is especially true of coins exhibiting mint luster or iridescent toning. Touching a bright copper surface with a sweaty thumb can easily result in a dark thumbprint several weeks or months later.

Thus, the first rule of handling coins is ***never touch a coin's obverse or reverse surface.*** If one needs to pick up a coin, touch only its edge. In the case of proof coins, even greater precaution must be taken. The reflective surfaces are so sensitive that one should avoid even breathing directly on a coin, which creates small black dots that coin collectors call "carbon spots." Also, do not expose coins to dust, sunlight, or wide changes in temperature.

SHOULD COINS BE CLEANED?

Many new collectors ask "How do I remove the toning?" It can be done, but it is not recommended. There are rare exceptions when cleaning a coin is beneficial, but in general, ***don't try it***. More harm than good will likely result. Toning is actually part of the coin. It is molecularly bonded to the metal, and the only way to remove the toning is to remove part of the coin. This is how most coin dips work, by means of a mild acid. Physical cleaning is even worse; microscopic striations in the coin's surface are usually the result.

COIN STORAGE

Coins can be stored in many ways. One of the most convenient methods is in two-inch square plastic "flips." These are transparent holders with two pockets—one for the coin and one for a cardboard ticket on which information can be recorded. It folds over into a size two inches by two inches. Originally, they were made of plastic containing polyvinylchloride. This material is particularly flexible and easy to work with, but eventually it breaks down, depositing a green slime on the coin in the holder.

Today, flips are made from a new, more inert Mylar formula and are available in addition to the old PVC flips. The Mylar type is prone to cracking, but so far has not been found to damage coins. The PVC type is still popular because it is more flexible, but it is usually used only by dealers and auction houses for temporary storage. Collectors usually repackage coins purchased in such holders for long-term storage.

Plastic "flips" are a common storage method for coins sold at shows and shops.

Cardboard 2-by-2 holders are also commonly used to store coins.

Another common coin holder is the "2-by-2." This is a pair of cardboard squares with an adhering film of relatively inert plastic on one side. The coin is sandwiched between the two layers of plastic, and the two halves are stapled together. This does not permit the coin to be removed and touched as easily as they can be in flips, but it does permit the coin to be viewed on both sides without opening the holder. When removing a coin from a 2-by-2, be careful not to scratch it on the exposed ends of the staples.

Flips and 2-by-2 holders fit nicely into specially made boxes. They also fit into plastic pages designed to hold 20 of either holder. The pages are transparent and will fit into most loose-leaf binders. It is important to remember not to place coins loose in the pages, which are often made of PVC plastic. Also, some of the thumb-cuts in the pockets for removing coins are large enough for some coins to fall through.

Many specialized coin folders and albums are designed not only to store and exhibit a collection but to guide collectors. The folder or album contains a labeled spot for each issue in a series. This basic format appeared on the original Whitman

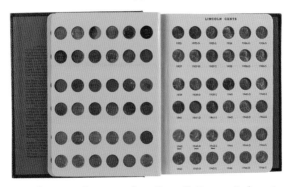

Coin albums provide storage and a guide to collecting a particular series.

"penny board" of the 1930s, which is widely credited with shaping coin collecting as it's practiced today.

Older folders and albums contained substances in the cardboard that toned the coins, although actual corrosion was rare. Today, most manufacturers omit these materials from their albums. Toning can occur on coins stored for the long term in orange-brown two-inch coin envelopes. Sulfur in the paper causes the toning.

It is best to store a coin collection in a cool, dry environment. Of course, not everyone lives in such a climate. One common solution to this is to store a packet of silica gel in the container with the coins. The gel is a desiccant and absorbs moisture from the air. It can sometimes be obtained at photo shops if not your local coin dealer.

ERROR COINS

An error is a coin manufactured incorrectly or one that is manufactured correctly on damaged or incorrectly made dies. Errors are attributed to a wide variety of mistakes, from the wrong metal being used to the coin being struck off center despite the U.S. Mint's attempts to limit errors or prevent them from entering circulation.

Because the modern automated manufacturing process creates far fewer errors and greater uniformity than older

1863 Indian Head Cent Struck Off Center.

methods, collectors of modern coins prize such mistakes. (Similar errors may actually reduce the value of ancient coins.) Errors in larger coins, proofs, and commemoratives tend to be scarcer because they are examined more closely before leaving the mint. Over the last 50 years, more have been getting out than in the past, and as a result, recent errors are not as valuable as early ones.

How each basic type of error occurs is explained following, along with the typical retail value for the error. Prices are for coins struck in the last 30 years. Actual examples may be worth more or less depending on the extent of the error. Values for most popular doubled-die cents appear in the regular listings.

Known Counterfeits: Most major doubled-die cents have been counterfeited. Virtually all examples of 1943 copper and

1944 steel cents are counterfeit. A magnet test will reveal deceptive plating but not cleverly altered dates. Also, it is easy to give the appearance of a mint error by striking a coin with another coin or hammering foreign matter into it. An apparent off-metal strike could have been plated after it was released from the mint. Some thin coins have been bathed in acid. (Is the surface abraded?) Clipped coins are easily confused with authentic clip errors. Almost all two-headed American coins are concoctions. Do not presume a coin is a mint error until you determine how it was made. There are thousands of such hoax coins out there.

(Values are for coins grading EF to MS-60.)

"BIE" Cent—A small chip out of the die between the letters "B" and "E" in "Liberty" looks like an extra letter "I." Fairly common in the 1950s. **25**
Blank—A blank, or planchet, is the piece of metal on which a coin is struck. Sometimes blanks escape the mint with no processing. Other times they escape unstruck but do make it through the machine that upsets the edge slightly. These are called type I and type II blanks, respectively.

Cent	.50	Nickel	2.50
Dime	2.00	Quarter	5.50
Half	17.00	Dollar	18.00

Brockage—Coin struck with a coin and a die instead of two dies. Caused by the previous coin adhering to one die. If it covers the whole die, it creates a "full brockage."

Cent	**13.50**	Nickel	**35.00**
Dime	**45.00**	Quarter	**45.00**
Half	**250.00**	Dollar	**250.00**

Clashed Dies—Coin struck with a die that has been previously struck by another die, leaving some of its impression behind. On the coin, the image of the primary die will be bold, and the image of the residual impression will be very faint.

Cent	**.75**	Nickel	**1.00**
Dime	**1.75**	Quarter	**4.00**
Half	**12.00**	Dollar	**30.00**

Clip (two types)—Coin struck on a blank that has part of its edge missing. There are two causes. A "regular clip" is caused by the punching device attempting to cut out the form of another coin before a previously punched blank is out of the way. A "straight clip" is caused when a blank is punched out too close to the end of the sheet of metal.

Cent	**.50**	Nickel	**2.50**
Dime	**2.00**	Quarter	**2.50**
Half	**10.00**	Dollar	**22.00**

Cud—A cud is a raised area of a coin near its edge. It is caused by a piece of the die chipping away. There is no striking surface in that spot to force the coin's metal down.

Cent	**1.00**	Nickel	**3.00**
Dime	**3.50**	Quarter	**6.50**
Half	**22.00**	Dollar	**35.00**

19??P Anthony Dollar with Cuds Caused by Chips from Edge of Die

Die Chip—A die chip is similar to a cud, but it can be very small and occur anywhere in the die, not just the edge.

Cent	**.25 to 1.00**	Nickel	**.25 to 3.00**
Dime	**.50 to 3.00**	Quarter	**2.00 to 6.00**
Half	**5.00 to 20.00**	Dollar	**5.00 to 30.00**

Die Crack—A crack in the die will cause a very fine raised line across the surface of the coin it strikes. Larger cracks are worth more than the values listed.

Cent	.50	Nickel	.75
Dime	.75	Quarter	1.50
Half	2.50	Dollar	6.00

Doubled Die—Caused by several errors in the manufacturing process. The coins will appear blurred at first glance, but upon closer inspection, the details appear to be doubled. *Prices vary widely, from $10 to $500 or more.*

*This 1955 Doubled-Die Lincoln Cent Is Worth
up to $1,500 in Circulated Grades*

Double Struck—When a coin that has been struck fails to eject from between the pair of dies, it will receive a second impression, usually not centered.

Cent	**10.00**	Nickel	**12.00**
Dime	**12.00**	Quarter	**40.00**
Half	**135.00**	Dollar	**400.00**

1886 Double Struck Indian Head Cent

Lamination—Occasionally called an "occluded gas lamination," this error is caused by improper mixture of metal when the alloy is being made. It will appear as flaking on the surface.

Cent	**.50**	Nickel	**3.00**
Dime	**4.00**	Quarter	**7.00**
Half	**12.00**	Dollar	**25.00**

Mismatched Dies—This occurs when one of the two dies is intended for another coin. To date, all but one has been struck on a blank intended for the larger coin.

Cent and Dime .... **two known**

Dollar and Quarter **47,500.00**

Off Center—When the blank is not lined up with the dies, only part of the impression is made. The other part of the blank remains just that—blank.

Cent	**1.00**	Nickel	**2.50**
Dime	**3.00**	Quarter	**8.00**
Half	**30.00**	Dollar	**40.00**

1904 Indian Head Cent Struck Off Center

Struck Through—A coin that had foreign matter on the blank, which was impressed into the surface by the die.

Cent	**1.50**	Nickel	**1.50**
Dime	**1.50**	Quarter	**3.50**
Half	**9.00**	Dollar	**11.00**

Wrong Metal—When a blank intended for one coin is accidentally mixed into blanks destined for another and is struck with those dies.

Cent	**100.00**	Nickel	**40.00**
Dime	**40.00**	Quarter	**45.00**
Half	**125.00**	Dollar	**375.00**

New York Statehood Quarter Struck on a Dime Planchet

U.S. COINS

HALF CENTS

Half cents are far more popular among collectors today than they were in circulation when issued. The small-denomination coins permitted precise dealings in commerce, but they were considered nuisances by those who had to handle them. Demand for half cents in circulation was low, which kept mintages low. In some years, none was struck. In other years, the U.S. Mint didn't allocate any blanks for them and struck them on second-hand merchant tokens instead.

Though not as popularly collected as large cents, half cents today are considered scarce and desirable. Like large cents, half cents are collected by die variety. Rare die combinations can be worth much more than common ones of the same year. Metal-detector finds exhibiting porous surfaces are worth substantially less than the prices listed. Early dates are difficult to find in better than well-worn condition. The Classic Head is much easier to find well preserved.

Known Counterfeits: Cheap cast replicas of the 1793 exist, as do more dangerous counterfeits of that date and the 1796 "no pole" variety. Dates on authentic half cents have been altered to resemble the rare 1831 date. The 1840s proof restrikes were struck by the U.S. Mint in the 1850s and 1860s.

1825 Half Cent with Classic Head

Classic Head	VG	VF
1809	78.00	100.00
1810	100.00	500.00
1811	375.00	1,800.00
1825	55.00	110.00
1826	65.00	90.00
1828	60.00	85.00
1829	70.00	100.00
1831	—	35,000.00
1831, restrike	—	6,500.00
1832	65.00	75.00
1833	65.00	75.00
1834	65.00	95.00
1835	65.00	75.00
1836, proof	—	6,000.00
1836, restrike proof	—	50,000.00

Braided Hair	VF	XF
1840, proof	—	3,000.00
1840, restrike proof	—	3,000.00
1841, proof	—	3,000.00
1841, restrike proof	—	3,000.00
1842, proof	—	3,000.00
1842, restrike proof	—	3,000.00
1843, proof	—	3,000.00

Braided Hair	VF	XF
1843, restrike proof	—	3,000.00
1844, proof	—	3,000.00
1844, restrike proof	—	3,000.00
1845, proof	—	3,000.00
1845, restrike proof	—	3,000.00
1846, proof	—	3,000.00
1846, restrike proof	—	3,000.00
1847, proof	—	3,000.00
1847, restrike proof	—	3,000.00
1848, proof	—	3,000.00
1848, restrike proof	—	3,000.00
1849, proof	—	3,000.00
1849, restrike proof	—	3,000.00
1849, large date	90.00	110.00
1850	90.00	110.00
1851	80.00	95.00
1852, proof	—	40,000.00
1852, restrike proof	—	3,000.00
1853	80.00	95.00
1854	80.00	95.00
1855	80.00	95.00
1856	80.00	95.00
1857	100.00	125.00

LARGE CENTS

The large cent resulted from the desire for a decimal coin worth one-hundredth of a dollar and the need for a coin to replace British halfpennies and their imitations, which had been common in the Colonies. It was slightly larger than the halfpenny, and the concept of decimal coinage was so innovative that the fraction "1/100" had to be written on the coin, along with the edge inscription "One Hundred for a Dollar."

The dies for striking early American coins were engraved by hand, so no two were identical. Because of this, collecting large cents by die variety is popular.

Low mintages and mediocre acceptance by the public caused the first large cents to be little more than local Philadelphia coinage. Metal was in such short supply that junked copper hardware of inconsistent alloy was used for some early cents, resulting in poor quality blanks on which to strike the coins. People also resented the chain on the first design of 1793 as a symbol antithetical to liberty and laughed at the frightened expression they perceived on Liberty's face.

Later, the coins became so popular that they were considered good luck. In the early 1800s, they were nailed to the rafters of new houses to bring good luck to its inhabitants. These old relics, found with characteristic square nail holes through them, have been nicknamed "rafter cents." Although their values are discounted, they still hold historical interest for collectors. Other large cents were stamped or hand engraved with advertising, personal initials, or risqué comments, and then placed back into circulation.

During the 1850s, dislike over the cent's size grew, and after eight years of research into smaller alternatives, the large cent was abandoned in 1857.

Rare die combinations can be worth much more than common ones of the same year. Metal-detector finds exhibiting porous surfaces are worth substantially less than the prices listed. Early dates are particularly difficult to find in better than well-worn condition.

Known Counterfeits: Large cents were not frequently counterfeited in their day. A few rarer dates were later counterfeited by casting (and possibly striking) to fool collectors. They include 1799, 1803, 1805 over 5, and 1851 over inverted 18. Some 1798 examples were altered to 1799. Some crude museum souvenirs chain cents also exist.

Coronet	VG	VF
1816	35.00	100.00
1817, 13 stars	35.00	75.00
1817, 15 stars	50.00	225.00
1818	30.00	70.00
1819	30.00	70.00

1828 Large Cent with Coronet

Coronet	VG	VF
1820	30.00	70.00
1821	75.00	400.00
1822	35.00	100.00
1823	200.00	690.00
1823, restrike	750.00	1,000.00
1824	35.00	180.00
1825	35.00	110.00
1826	35.00	85.00
1827	35.00	90.00
1828	35.00	90.00
1829	35.00	90.00
1830	30.00	70.00
1831	30.00	70.00

1833 Large Cent with Coronet

Coronet	VG	VF
1832	30.00	70.00
1833	30.00	70.00
1834	30.00	70.00
1835	30.00	70.00
1836	30.00	70.00
1837	30.00	70.00
1838	30.00	70.00
1839	35.00	80.00

Braided Hair	VG	VF
1840	30.00	35.00
1841	30.00	40.00
1842	30.00	35.00
1843	30.00	35.00
1844	30.00	35.00
1845	30.00	35.00
1846	25.00	35.00
1847	25.00	35.00
1848	30.00	35.00
1849	30.00	35.00
1850	30.00	35.00
1851	25.00	35.00
1852	25.00	35.00
1853	25.00	35.00

1840 Large Cent with Braided Hair

Braided Hair	VG	VF
1854	25.00	35.00
1855	30.00	35.00
1856	30.00	35.00
1857	125.00	210.00

FLYING EAGLE CENTS

After years of experimenting, the Mint introduced a small cent in 1857. It was less than half the weight of the large cent and was brown to beige in color, thanks to its alloy of 88-percent copper and 12-percent nickel. It depicted an eagle flying left, modeled after "Old Pete," a bird that years earlier had served as a mascot at the Mint. Its wreath on the reverse includes tobacco leaves.

Some Flying Eagle cents initially were released at below face value to encourage their acceptance, but the old large cents were so bulky that it didn't take people long to accept the new coins. The 1856 is technically a pattern but was widely distributed at the time and is generally collected as part of the series.

Known Counterfeits: Many 1856 cents encountered are counterfeit. They are usually made from authentic coins with the dates re-engraved.

1858 Flying Eagle Cent

Flying Eagle	VG	VF
1856	7,250.00	10,750.00
1857	40.00	45.00
1858, large letters	40.00	55.00
1858, small letters	40.00	50.00

INDIAN HEAD CENTS

Indian Head cent legend is one of numismatics' most charming stories. According to the story, U.S. Mint engraver James B. Longacre was entertaining an Indian chief who happened to be wearing his full war bonnet. As a gesture of whimsy, the chief removed his bonnet and placed it on the head of Longacre's young daughter, Sarah. Legend says the engraver instantly perceived that this was the image destined for the next American cent. Admittedly, fewer people believe the tale as time goes on, but it does add a quaint bit of sentimentality to the origin of one of America's favorite coin designs.

When the Indian Head cent was first released, it was struck in the same copper-nickel alloy as the Flying Eagle cent. The reverse was a simple laurel wreath encircling the words "One Cent." The following year, the laurel wreath was replaced by an oak wreath, often considered a symbol of authority, with a bundle of arrows tied at the bottom. Its top was open enough to fit a small American shield.

In 1864, nickel was removed from the alloy, giving the coin the bronze appearance that has since characterized the U.S. cent. It was also made thinner. This new bronze cent was reminiscent of the private one-cent Civil War tokens that circulated at the time and cost a fraction of a cent to manufacture.

Known Counterfeits: Struck counterfeits of the 1867, 1868, open-3 1873, and 1877 exist. Counterfeits of the 1908S and 1909S are often made by altering authentic 1908 and 1909 Indian cents.

Copper-Nickel Alloy	F	XF
1859	20.00	100.00

1859 Indian Head Cent

Copper-Nickel Alloy	F	XF
1860	20.00	70.00
1861	40.00	95.00
1862	10.00	30.00
1863	10.00	25.00
1864	35.00	125.00

Bronze	F	XF
1864	25.00	70.00
1864, "L" on ribbon	140.00	275.00
1865	20.00	40.00
1866	80.00	200.00
1867	110.00	200.00
1868	75.00	180.00
1869	230.00	450.00
1870	225.00	410.00
1871	280.00	420.00
1872	390.00	625.00
1873	40.00	155.00
1874	45.00	110.00
1875	55.00	120.00
1876	75.00	230.00
1877	1,475.00	2,600.00
1878	70.00	245.00
1879	16.00	75.00

Bronze	F	XF
1880	7.00	30.00
1881	7.00	20.00
1882	5.00	20.00
1883	5.00	15.00
1884	7.00	30.00
1885	10.00	60.00
1886	20.00	150.00
1887	4.00	20.00
1888	5.00	20.00
1889	3.00	12.00
1890	3.00	10.00
1891	3.00	13.00
1892	4.50	18.00
1893	3.25	10.00
1894	13.00	50.00
1895	3.50	11.00
1896	3.25	13.00
1897	2.75	10.00
1898	2.75	10.00
1899	2.50	10.00
1900	2.50	12.00
1901	2.50	11.00
1902	2.50	10.00

1882 Bronze Indian Head Cent

1902 Bronze Indian Head Cent

Bronze	F	XF
1903	2.50	10.00
1904	2.50	10.00
1905	2.50	9.00
1906	2.50	9.00
1907	2.50	8.50
1908	2.50	9.00
1908S	70.00	160.00
1909	15.00	30.00
1909S	585.00	720.00

LINCOLN CENTS

The Lincoln cent was the first regular issue U.S. coin to bear the portrait of a real person. It was issued to celebrate the centennial of Abraham Lincoln's birth. It was designed by Victor David Brenner, a sculptor from outside the Mint's staff. His initials are found prominently on the reverses of the first examples released. Some thought they were featured too prominently, and the outcry forced their removal, causing two varieties for the first year. Later in 1918, they were added more discretely under the truncation of the shoulder.

Lincoln cents were a bronze alloy of 95-percent copper until 1943, when they were changed to zinc-coated steel to save copper for the war effort. Because sometimes the steel cents were confused with dimes, they were replaced in 1944 and 1945 with cents made from melted spent shell casings, resulting in a much more conventional appearance.

The original alloy was restored from 1946 until 1982, when it was finally abandoned for copper-plated zinc to reduce production costs. If you cut one of the current cents in half, it will not be orange or brown inside but white, revealing its true composition.

A new reverse, depicting the Lincoln Memorial in Washington D.C., was introduced in 1959 to commemorate the 150th anniversary of Lincoln's birth. The Lincoln cent reverse was scheduled to change again in 2009 to commemorate the bicentennial of Lincoln's birth. A law passed Sept. 27, 2006, requires the U.S. Mint to strike 2009-dated circulating Lincoln cents with four different reverse designs emblematic of various stages of Lincoln's life: (1) his birth and early childhood in Kentucky, (2) his formative years in Indiana, (3) his professional life in Illinois, and (4) his presidency. The law further mandates that after 2009 the Lincoln cent reverse design will represent Lincoln's "preservation of the United States of America as a single and united country." The law also mandates that Brenner's obverse design continue to be used.

The Lincoln cent is one of the most popularly collected coins. It is collected in most grades, and even the rarities can be found without too much searching of dealers' inventories and advertisements.

Known Counterfeits: The 1909S VDB, 1909S, 1914D, 1922 plain, 1931S, and 1955 doubled-die Lincoln cents have been extensively counterfeited. Most are altered cents of other dates. Counterfeits of the 1972 doubled die also exist. Virtually all 1943 bronze and 1944 steel cents are counterfeit. A magnet test will reveal the crudest counterfeits made by plating. Other 1943 bronze cents have been made by altering 1948 cents and by striking with false dies.

In addition to counterfeits, the collector should be aware of "reprocessed" cents. These are circulated 1943 steel cents given a fresh zinc coating to make them appear uncirculated. Many hobbyists are quite willing to have them in their collections, but it is important to know the difference. Don't look for luster, but rather for traces of flatness at the cheekbone.

Wheat Ears Reverse	VF	MS-60
1909 VDB	13.00	20.00
1909S VDB	1,150.00	1,650.00
1909	5.00	15.00
1909S	170.00	360.00
1910	1.50	17.50
1910S	30.00	105.00
1911	2.50	20.00
1911D	18.50	90.00

1909S VDB Lincoln Cent with Wheat Ears Reverse

Wheat Ears Reverse	VF	MS-60
1911S	55.00	180.00
1912	6.00	35.00
1912D	27.00	165.00
1912S	40.00	185.00
1913	3.50	35.00
1913D	11.00	100.00
1913S	30.00	195.00
1914	6.50	50.00
1914D	500.00	1,975.00
1914S	40.00	300.00
1915	20.00	85.00
1915D	6.75	70.00
1915S	30.00	175.00
1916	2.50	18.00
1916D	6.00	70.00
1916S	7.00	85.00
1917	2.00	16.00
1917D	5.50	60.00
1917S	2.50	60.00
1918	1.25	15.00
1918D	5.50	70.00
1918S	3.50	60.00
1919	.80	8.50

1922 Plain (No D) Lincoln Cent with Wheat Ears Reverse

Wheat Ears Reverse	VF	MS-60
1919D	5.00	55.00
1919S	2.50	40.00
1920	1.50	14.00
1920D	7.00	75.00
1920S	2.75	110.00
1921	3.00	45.00
1921S	6.00	110.00
1922D	25.00	110.00
1922, plain	1,700.00	11,000.00
1923	1.50	14.00
1923S	8.00	195.00
1924	1.10	20.00
1924D	60.00	270.00
1924S	5.00	115.00
1925	.70	10.00
1925D	6.00	60.00
1925S	3.00	90.00
1926	.70	8.00
1926D	5.50	85.00
1926S	15.00	140.00
1927	.70	7.50
1927D	3.50	65.00
1927S	4.65	65.00

Wheat Ears Reverse	VF	MS-60
1928	.70	7.50
1928D	3.75	35.00
1928S	4.00	75.00
1929	.60	7.00
1929D	2.85	25.00
1929S	3.00	20.00
1930	.60	4.00
1930D	.90	11.00
1930S	.80	10.00
1931	2.00	20.00
1931D	8.00	50.00
1931S	140.00	165.00
1932	3.50	20.00
1932D	2.85	17.50
1933	3.00	17.50
1933D	6.50	23.00
1934	.60	8.00
1934D	1.65	20.00
1935	.50	3.50
1935D	.40	4.50
1935S	1.75	12.00
1936	.55	2.00
1936D	.55	3.50

1932D Lincoln Cent with Wheat Ears Reverse

Wheat Ears Reverse	VF	MS-60
1936S	.60	3.00
1937	.55	1.60
1937D	.60	2.20
1937S	.55	2.50
1938	.55	3.00
1938D	.60	3.50
1938S	.70	2.80
1939	.55	1.00
1939D	.60	2.25
1939S	.60	2.00
1940	.40	1.00
1940D	.55	1.20
1940S	.55	1.25
1941	.40	.85
1941D	.55	2.25
1941S	.55	2.25
1942	.40	.85
1942D	.35	.65
1942S	.85	4.50
1943, steel	.45	1.25
1943D, steel	.50	1.25
1943S, steel	.65	3.00
1944	.20	.60

1943S Lincoln cents were produced in zinc-coated steel during World War II.

Wheat Ears Reverse	VF	MS-60
1944D	.20	.85
1944, D over S	160.00	375.00
1944S	.20	.65
1945	.20	1.25
1945D	.20	1.25
1945S	.20	.65
1946	.20	.50
1946D	.20	.50
1946S	.20	.50
1947	.20	1.50
1947D	.20	.50
1947S	.20	.55
1948	.20	.60
1948D	.20	.70
1948S	.20	1.35
1951D	.20	.50
1951S	.20	.90
1952	.20	1.40
1952D	.20	.50
1952S	.30	2.00
1953	.20	.50
1953D	.20	.50

Wheat Ears Reverse	VF	MS-60
1953S	.20	.60
1954	.20	.40
1954D	.20	.40
1954S	.20	.40
1955	.20	.40
1955, doubled die	1,450.00	2,050.00
1955, minor date shift or ("poor man's doubled die")	.20	.40
1955D	.20	.40
1955S	.30	.60
1956	.15	.30
1956D	.20	.30
1957	.20	.30
1957D	.20	.30
1958	.20	.30
1958D	.20	.30

Lincoln Memorial Reverse	MS-65
1959	18.00
1959D	16.00
1960, large date	10.00
1960, small date	12.00
1960D, large date	11.00

Lincoln Memorial Reverse	MS-65
1960D, small date	10.00
1961	6.50
1961D	15.00
1962	8.00
1962D	14.00
1963	10.00
1963D	12.00
1964	6.50
1964D	7.00
1965	10.00
1966	10.00
1967	10.00
1968	12.00
1968D	12.00
1968S	8.00
1969	6.50
1969D	10.00
1969S	8.00
1970	8.00
1970D	6.00
1970S, small date	75.00
1970S, large date	16.00

1964D Lincoln Cent with Lincoln Memorial Reverse

Lincoln Memorial Reverse	MS-65
1971	25.00
1971D	5.50
1971S	6.00
1972	6.00
1972, doubled die	775.00
1972D	10.00
1972S	30.00
1973	8.00
1973D	11.00
1973S	8.00
1974	12.00
1974D	12.00
1974S	10.00
1975	8.00
1975D	13.50
1975S, proof	5.50
1976	18.00
1976D	20.00
1976S, proof	5.00
1977	14.00
1977D	14.00

Lincoln Memorial Reverse	MS-65
1977S, proof	3.00
1978	14.00
1978D	12.00
1978S, proof	3.50
1979	12.00
1979D	8.00
1979S, proof	4.00
1980	6.50
1980D	10.00
1980S, proof	2.25
1981	7.50
1981D	9.00
1981S, proof	3.50
1982	6.00
1982D	6.00
1982S, proof	3.00

Copper-Plated Zinc	MS-65
1982	6.00
1982D	6.00
1983	7.00
1983, doubled die reverse	400.00

1982S Lincoln Cent with Lincoln Memorial Reverse

Copper-Plated Zinc	MS-65
1983D	5.50
1983S, proof	4.00
1984	7.50
1984, doubled die	275.00
1984D	5.50
1984S, proof	4.50
1985	4.50
1985D	4.50
1985S, proof	6.00
1986	5.00
1986D	8.00
1986S, proof	7.50
1987	8.50
1987D	6.00
1987S, proof	5.00
1988	8.50
1988D	5.50
1988S, proof	4.00
1989	5.00
1989D	5.00
1989S, proof	6.00
1990	5.00

Copper-Plated Zinc	MS-65
1990D	5.00
1990S, proof	5.00
1990S, without S, proof	2,750.00
1991	6.00
1991D	5.00
1991S, proof	5.00
1992	5.50
1992D	5.50
1992S, proof	5.00
1993	5.50
1993D	5.50
1993S, proof	7.00
1994	10.00
1994D	5.50
1994S, proof	4.00
1995	4.50
1995, doubled die	50.00
1995D	5.50
1995S, proof	9.50
1996	5.00
1996D	5.00
1996S, proof	6.50

*1990S Proof Lincoln Cent Error (Coin Struck at
San Francisco Mint without S Mark)*

Copper-Plated Zinc	MS-65
1997	5.00
1997D	5.00
1997S, proof	11.50
1998	5.00
1998D	5.00
1998S, proof	9.50
1999	5.00
1999D	5.00
1999S, proof	5.00
2000	4.00
2000D	4.00
2000S, proof	4.00
2001	4.00
2001D	4.00
2001S, proof	4.00
2002	4.00
2002D	4.00
2002S, proof	4.00

Copper-Plated Zinc	MS-65
2003	3.50
2003D	3.50
2003S, proof	4.00
2004	3.50
2004D	3.50
2004S, proof	4.00
2005	3.50
2005D	3.50
2005S, proof	4.00
2006	2.00
2006D	2.50
2006S, proof	4.00
2007	1.50
2007D	1.50
2007S, proof	4.00
2008	1.50
2008D	1.50
2008S	4.00

2009 Lincoln Cent Reverse (1.) Birth and Childhood in Kentucky

2009 Lincoln Cent Reverse (2.) Formative Years in Indiana

2009 Lincoln Cent Reverse (3.) Professional Life in Illinois

2009 Lincoln Cent Reverse (4.) Presidency

TWO-CENT PIECES

Americans hoarded coins throughout the Civil War. They preferred to spend the less valuable private tokens and small-denomination paper money. If the North fell, they thought, then at least real coins would retain some value. A shortage of small change resulted. The two-cent piece was introduced in an attempt to alleviate this shortage. It was the first coin to carry the inscription "In God We Trust."

Two-cent pieces are usually found well worn; fewer than one in a hundred survive in Fine or better.

Known Counterfeits: Counterfeits are not particularly common, though some scarce die-struck ones are known.

	F	XF
1864, small motto (open D in God)	265.00	595.00
1864, large motto (narrow D in God)	22.00	40.00
1865	22.00	40.00
1866	23.00	40.00
1867	36.00	60.00
1868	38.00	63.00
1869	40.00	70.00
1870	45.00	115.00
1871	55.00	130.00
1872	470.00	850.00
1873, proof	1,500.00	1,750.00

1867 Two-Cent Piece

SILVER THREE-CENT PIECES

Different times have different priorities, and the reasons for striking coins in one era don't always seem to make sense to the people living in another. This is the case with the silver three-cent piece, often called the "trime." This small coin and the gold $3 were issued to make it easier to purchase three-cent first-class postage stamps in singles and sheets. Despite their small size, they were accepted enough in commerce that they continued to be struck in significant quantities for 12 years.

The coin's thinness prevented it from striking well, and the Mint attempted to modify its design repeatedly. Finding a fully struck coin with no weak spots, even in higher grades, is difficult. The thin coin is also susceptible to bending, dents, and crinkling. Prices given are for flat, undamaged examples.

Known Counterfeits: Counterfeits dated 1860 and 1861 made to pass in circulation were struck in base silver and white metal. Struck counterfeits of the 1864 also exist.

No Border Around Star	F	XF
1851	43.00	65.00
18510	55.00	160.00
1852	43.00	65.00
1853	43.00	65.00

Triple Border Around Star	F	XF
1854	44.00	105.00
1855	75.00	205.00
1856	46.00	125.00
1857	45.00	130.00
1858	44.00	110.00

Double Border Around Star	F	XF
1859	50.00	83.00
1860	45.00	80.00
1861	45.00	80.00
1862	50.00	83.00
1863	400.00	480.00
1864	400.00	480.00
1865	475.00	550.00
1866	400.00	495.00
1867	475.00	550.00
1868	480.00	575.00
1869	480.00	575.00
1870	495.00	595.00
1871	480.00	575.00
1872	495.00	595.00
1873, proof	730.00	890.00

1863 Silver Three-Cent Piece with Double Border Around Star

NICKEL THREE-CENT PIECES

The tiny silver three-cent piece served a purpose, but its size was impractical. Because silver was hoarded during the Civil War, a convenient non-silver coin of this value was needed. The three-cent coin was thus made bigger and changed to an alloy of 75-percent copper and 25-percent nickel, just enough nickel to give it a white color. Despite their active use in commerce for decades, well-preserved examples are easy to find.

Known Counterfeits: Few if any counterfeits of this coin are known.

	F	XF
1865	18.00	35.00
1866	18.00	35.00
1867	18.00	35.00
1868	18.00	35.00
1869	20.00	40.00
1870	21.00	40.00
1871	23.00	42.00
1872	25.00	44.00
1873	23.00	40.00
1874	23.00	42.00
1875	30.00	45.00

1865 Nickel Three-Cent Piece

	F	XF
1876	25.00	50.00
1877, proof	1,175.00	1,300.00
1878, proof	720.00	795.00
1879	96.00	115.00
1880	130.00	185.00
1881	19.00	40.00
1882	180.00	300.00
1883	260.00	375.00
1884	550.00	645.00
1885	645.00	745.00
1886, proof	345.00	385.00
1887	395.00	455.00
1888	70.00	100.00
1889	140.00	220.00

LIBERTY NICKELS

Liberty nickels had one of the most controversial beginnings of all American coins. The original design had the denomination of five cents indicated simply by the Roman numeral V without the word "Cents." Some unprincipled persons gold plated these coins and passed them off as the new gold $5 coin. These plated frauds became known as "racketeer nickels" and prompted an immediate change in the coin's design. The word "Cents" was added boldly underneath the large V.

Today, racketeer nickels have some value as collector novelties but not as much as an original, unaltered example. Interestingly, the original "no cents" nickel is quite common today in medium to high grades, perhaps because it was saved as a novelty in its day.

The famous 1913 Liberty nickel is not an authorized issue but was struck by a scheming Mint employee with an eye to profit. The first advertisements to purchase these rare coins were placed by the original seller to excite interest in the numismatic community, but he knew no other examples existed. Today, the known examples of the 1913 Liberty nickel are some of the most valuable coins in the world.

Known Counterfeits: There are counterfeits of the 1913, but they cause few problems because all five authentic pieces are in known hands. There are 1912S counterfeits made from altered 1912D nickels.

1883 Liberty Nickel (without "Cents" below "V")

	F	XF
1883, without "Cents"	7.00	8.00
1883, with "Cents"	42.00	90.00
1884	42.00	95.00
1885	900.00	1,350.00
1886	425.00	715.00
1887	35.00	85.00
1888	70.00	185.00
1889	30.00	85.00
1890	28.00	70.00
1891	22.00	65.00
1892	23.00	65.00
1893	25.00	65.00
1894	100.00	240.00
1895	25.00	70.00

	F	XF
1896	40.00	100.00
1897	13.00	45.00
1898	11.00	40.00
1899	8.50	35.00
1900	8.50	35.00
1901	7.00	35.00
1902	4.50	30.00
1903	5.00	30.00
1904	5.00	30.00
1905	4.50	30.00
1906	4.50	30.00
1907	4.50	30.00
1908	4.50	30.00
1909	4.50	30.00
1910	4.50	30.00
1911	4.50	30.00
1912	4.50	30.00
1912D	12.00	75.00
1912S	280.00	850.00
1913, proof, five known	—	March 2001 auction, $1.84 million

1896 Liberty Nickel

1907 Liberty Nickel

BUFFALO NICKELS

The Buffalo nickel, also and more appropriately called the Indian Head nickel, was one of the most artistically progressive American coins to have been struck when first issued. It was designed by James Earle Fraser, a noted sculptor of the era. Traditional belief holds that three different Indians posed for the obverse portrait, but this theory has recently been called into question.

The original reverse depicting an American bison standing on a mound was changed because the words "Five Cents" were in such high relief that they would quickly wear off. The second reverse has the denomination in a recess below a plane on which the bison stands. The date is rendered in high relief on these coins as well and is usually worn off on coins grading below very good. These "dateless" coins are of little value.

One entertaining sidelight to the Buffalo nickel is the hobo nickel. During the Great Depression, hobos and other individuals re-engraved the obverse portrait on the coins and then tried to sell them for more than face value to earn some pocket money. These re-engraved coins are considered folk art today, and some individual artists have been identified.

Known Counterfeits: The 1937D "three-legged" variety is the most counterfeited coin in the series. Counterfeits of this variety have numerous minor design details missing. Other common counterfeits are authentic coins altered to appear to be the 1913S Type II, 1918/7D, 1921S, 1924S, 1926D, and 1926S.

	F	MS-60
1913, bison on mound	12.00	35.00
1913D, bison on mound	20.00	65.00
1913S, bison on mound	50.00	125.00
1913, bison on line	11.50	35.00
1913D, bison on line	180.00	285.00
1913S, bison on line	445.00	850.00
1914	22.00	50.00
1914D	155.00	450.00
1914S	45.00	160.00
1915	8.00	50.00
1915D	40.00	225.00
1915S	105.00	625.00
1916	7.00	45.00
1916D	30.00	150.00
1916S	20.00	175.00
1917	8.00	60.00
1917D	55.00	345.00
1917S	80.00	400.00
1918	8.00	110.00
1918, 8 over 7	2,850.00	28,500.00
1918D	65.00	430.00
1918S	55.00	500.00
1919	4.00	60.00

1913D Buffalo Nickel

	F	MS-60
1919D	65.00	570.00
1919S	50.00	540.00
1920	3.25	60.00
1920D	35.00	555.00
1920S	30.00	525.00
1921	8.50	125.00
1921S	200.00	1,500.00
1923	4.25	60.00
1923S	25.00	600.00
1924	4.50	75.00
1924D	30.00	375.00
1924S	96.00	2,300.00
1925	3.75	45.00
1925D	40.00	380.00
1925S	17.50	440.00
1926	3.00	30.00
1926D	30.00	315.00
1926S	100.00	5,000.00
1927	2.50	35.00
1927D	7.00	150.00
1927S	6.00	485.00
1928	2.50	35.00
1928D	4.00	50.00

1937D "Three-Legged" Buffalo

	F	MS-60
1928S	3.00	215.00
1929	2.50	35.00
1929D	3.00	55.00
1929S	2.25	50.00
1930	2.50	35.00
1930S	3.00	55.00
1931S	20.00	65.00
1934	2.50	50.00
1934D	4.75	85.00

	F	MS-60
1935	2.25	20.00
1935D	3.00	75.00
1935S	2.50	50.00
1936	2.25	15.00
1936D	2.75	35.00
1936S	2.50	35.00
1937	2.25	15.00
1937D	2.50	30.00
1937D, three-legged	950.00	2,700.00
1937S	2.50	30.00
1938D	4.00	20.00
1938D, D over S	10.00	50.00

JEFFERSON NICKELS

The Jefferson nickel was the first circulating U.S. coin to be designed by public contest. Felix Schlag won $1,000 for his design featuring Jefferson's portrait on one side and his home, Monticello, on the other. The initial rendition lacks the designer's initials, which were added in 1966.

Because it is difficult to get the metal to flow into every crevice of the die, the steps leading up to Monticello are incompletely struck on many Jefferson nickels. "Full step" nickels sometimes command a premium from specialists.

During World War II, nickel was needed for the war effort, so from mid-1942 to the end of 1945 "nickels" were struck in an unusual alloy of 56-percent copper, 35-percent silver and nine-percent manganese. These "war nickels" bear a large mintmark over the dome of Monticello on the reverse. They exhibited great brilliance when new, but quickly turned an ugly dull color with a moderate amount of wear.

Congress authorized new nickel designs for 2004 and 2005 to commemorate the bicentennial of Lewis and Clark's exploration of the Louisiana Territory. As president, Thomas Jefferson authorized the mission to find the "most direct and practicable water communication across this continent for the purpose of commerce." For 2006, an image of Jefferson based on a Rembrandt Peale portrait from 1800 was used on the obverse.

Known Counterfeits: 1950D. Crude casts were also made to circulate in the 1940s.

Copper-Nickel Alloy	VF	MS-60
1938	1.00	6.00
1938D	1.50	10.00
1938S	2.50	5.25
1939	.25	1.75
1939D	8.00	45.00

1939 Jefferson Nickel

Copper-Nickel Alloy	VF	MS-60
1939S	1.50	17.00
1940	.25	1.00
1940D	.30	1.50
1940S	.25	2.50
1941	.25	.75
1941D	.30	2.50
1941S	.30	3.75
1942	.25	5.00
1942D	3.00	32.00

Copper-Silver-Manganese Alloy	VF	MS-60
1942P	1.50	8.00
1942S	1.50	14.00
1943P	1.50	4.00
1943P, 3 over 2	75.00	250.00
1943D	1.70	5.00
1943S	1.50	6.00
1944P	1.50	10.00
1944D	1.50	10.00
1944S	1.50	7.00
1945P	1.50	6.00
1945D	1.60	5.50
1945S	1.50	5.00

1943P Jefferson Nickel with Copper-Silver-Manganese Alloy

Copper-Nickel Alloy	VF	MS-60
1946	.20	.80
1946D	.25	1.00
1946S	.30	.50
1947	.20	.75
1947D	.20	.90
1947S	.20	1.00
1948	.20	.50
1948D	.25	1.20
1948S	.25	1.20
1949	.25	2.25
1949D	.30	1.25
1949D, D over S	40.00	170.00
1949S	.45	1.50

Copper-Nickel Alloy	VF	MS-60
1950	.35	1.50
1950D	13.00	16.00
1951	.40	1.50
1951D	.40	3.00
1951S	.50	1.75
1952	.20	.85
1952D	.30	2.00
1952S	.20	.75
1953	.20	.40
1953D	.20	.40
1953S	.20	.60
1954	.20	.60
1954D	.20	.35
1954S	.25	1.00
1954S, S over D	14.00	50.00
1955	.40	.75
1955D	—	.20
1955D, D over S	16.00	65.00
1956	—	.30
1956D	—	.25
1957	—	.25
1957D	—	.25
1958	.15	.30

Copper-Nickel Alloy	MS-65
1958D	.30
1959	.30
1959D	.25
1960	.30
1960D	.30
1961	.25
1961D	.25
1962	.25
1962D	.25
1963	.25
1963D	.25
1964	.25
1964D	.25
1965	.25
1966	.25
1967	.25
1968D	.25
1968S	.50
1969D	.50
1969S	.50
1970D	.50
1970S	.50

1965 Jefferson Nickel

Copper-Nickel Alloy	MS-65
1971	2.00
1971D	.50
1971S, proof	2.00
1972	.50
1972D	.50
1972S, proof	2.00
1973	.50
1973D	.50
1973S, proof	1.75
1974	.50
1974D	.50
1974S, proof	2.00
1975	.75
1975D	.50
1975S, proof	2.25
1976	.75
1976D	.60
1976S, proof	2.00
1977	.40
1977D	.55
1977S, proof	1.75
1978	.40
1978D	.40

Copper-Nickel Alloy	MS-65
1978S, proof	1.75
1979	.40
1979D	.40
1979S, proof	1.50
1980P	.40
1980D	.40
1980S, proof	1.50
1981P	.40
1981D	.40
1981S, proof	2.00
1982P	13.00
1982D	3.50
1982S, proof	3.00
1983P	4.00
1983D	2.50
1983S, proof	4.00
1984P	3.00
1984D	.85
1984S, proof	5.00
1985P	.75
1985D	.75
1985S, proof	4.00
1986P	1.00

Copper-Nickel Alloy	MS-65
1986D	2.00
1986S, proof	7.00
1987P	.75
1987D	.75
1987S, proof	3.50
1988P	.75
1988D	.75
1988S, proof	6.50
1989P	.75
1989D	.75
1989S, proof	5.50
1990P	.75
1990D	.75
1990S, proof	5.50
1991P	.75
1991D	.75
1991S, proof	5.00
1992P	2.00
1992D	.75
1992S, proof	4.00
1993P	.75
1993D	.75
1993S, proof	4.50

Copper-Nickel Alloy	MS-65
1994P	.75
1994P, matte proof	75.00
1994D	.75
1994S, proof	4.00
1995P	.75
1995D	.85
1995S, proof	4.00
1996P	.75
1996D	.75
1996S, proof	4.00
1997P	.75
1997P, matte proof	200.00
1997D	2.00
1997S, proof	5.00
1998P	.80
1998D	.80
1998S, proof	4.50
1999P	.80
1999D	.80
1999S, proof	3.50
2000P	.80
2000D	.80
2000S, proof	2.00

Copper-Nickel Alloy	MS-65
2001P	.50
2001D	.50
2001S, proof	2.00
2002P	.50
2002D	.50
2002S, proof	2.00
2003P	.50
2003D	.50
2003S, proof	2.00
2004P, peace-medal reverse	1.00
2004D, peace-medal reverse	1.00
2004S, peace-medal reverse, proof	13.00
2004P, keelboat reverse	1.00
2004D, keelboat reverse	1.00
2004S, keelboat reverse, proof	13.00

2004D Jefferson Nickel with Peace Reverse

2004D Jefferson Nickel with Lewis and Clark Keelboat Reverse

Copper-Nickel Alloy	MS-65
2005P, bison reverse	1.00
2005D, bison reverse	1.00
2005S, bison reverse, proof	7.50
2005P, "Ocean in View!" reverse	1.00
2005D, "Ocean in View!" reverse	1.00
2005S, "Ocean in View!," proof	6.50
2006P	1.00
2006D	1.00
2006S, proof	4.00
2007P	1.00
2007D	1.00
2007S, proof	4.00
2008P	1.00
2008D	1.00
2008S, proof	4.00

2005D Jefferson Nickel with Bison Reverse

2005D Jefferson Nickel with "Ocean in View" Reverse

2006D Jefferson Nickel with Jefferson, 1800
Obverse/Return to Monticello Reverse

SEATED LIBERTY HALF DIMES

Following the introduction of Christian Gobrecht's Seated Liberty design on the silver dollar, smaller coins gradually adapted this design. The half dime and dime, because of their small size, depicted a laurel wreath encircling the denomination on the reverse, rather than an eagle.

Several minor changes were introduced over the life of this coin. After only a year, the plain obverse was ornamented by 13 stars. Two years later, additional drapery was added below Liberty's elbow. The arrows by the date from 1853 to 1855 indicate a 7.5-percent reduction in weight. A far more obvious design change was the shift of the words "United States of America" from the reverse to the obverse in 1860.

The Seated Liberty half dime's thinness resulted in frequent bending and dents. Prices given are for flat, undamaged examples.

Known Counterfeits: Counterfeit half dimes are not frequently encountered.

Plain Obverse	VG	VF
1837	45.00	135.00
18380	130.00	475.00

1837 Seated Liberty Half Dime with Plain Obverse Field

Stars On Obverse	VG	VF
1838	25.00	35.00
1839	25.00	35.00
1839O	30.00	40.00
1840	25.00	40.00
1840O	30.00	50.00
1841	20.00	30.00
1841O	25.00	50.00
1842	20.00	30.00
1842O	45.00	225.00
1843	20.00	30.00
1844	25.00	35.00
1844O	110.00	600.00
1845	20.00	35.00
1846	550.00	1,250.00
1847	20.00	30.00
1848	25.00	35.00
1848O	25.00	65.00
1849	20.00	50.00
1849O	40.00	225.00
1849/8	35.00	70.00
1850	25.00	35.00
1850O	25.00	65.00
1851	20.00	30.00
1851O	25.00	40.00

18550 Seated Liberty Half Dime with
Stars and Arrows on Obverse

Stars On Obverse	VG	VF
1852	20.00	30.00
1852O	45.00	135.00
1853, no arrows at date	60.00	175.00
1853O, no arrows at date	325.00	850.00
1853, arrows at date	20.00	30.00
1853O, arrows at date	25.00	35.00
1854	20.00	30.00
1854O	20.00	40.00
1855	20.00	30.00
1855O	20.00	55.00
1856	20.00	35.00
1856O	20.00	30.00
1857	20.00	30.00
1857O	20.00	30.00
1858	20.00	30.00
1858O	20.00	30.00
1859	25.00	30.00
1859O	25.00	40.00

Legend On Obverse	VG	VF
1860	20.00	25.00
1861	20.00	25.00
1862	25.00	45.00
1863	250.00	400.00

1863 Seated Liberty Half Dime with Legend on Obverse

Legend On Obverse	VG	VF
1863S	45.00	95.00
1864	475.00	750.00
1864S	75.00	175.00
1865	475.00	750.00
1865S	40.00	85.00
1866	475.00	700.00
1866S	40.00	85.00
1867	650.00	900.00
1867S	40.00	85.00
1868	90.00	225.00
1868S	25.00	40.00
1869	25.00	40.00
1869S	25.00	35.00
1870	25.00	35.00
1870S, unique	—	July 1986 auction, $235,000
1871	20.00	25.00
1871S	30.00	60.00
1872	20.00	25.00
1872S	20.00	25.00
1873	20.00	25.00
1873S	25.00	40.00

SEATED LIBERTY DIMES

Following the introduction of Christian Gobrecht's Seated Liberty design on the silver dollar, smaller coins gradually adapted this design. The dime and half dime, because of their small size, depicted a laurel wreath encircling the denomination on the reverse, rather than an eagle.

There were several minor changes over the life of this coin. After slightly more than a year, the plain obverse was ornamented by 13 stars. A year later, additional drapery was added below Liberty's elbow. The arrows by the date from 1853 to 1855 indicate a seven-percent reduction in weight. Arrows by the date in 1873 and 1874 indicate a minuscule increase in weight. A more obvious design change was the shift of the words "United States Of America" from the reverse to the obverse in 1860.

The Seated Liberty dime's thinness resulted in frequent bending and dents. Prices given are for flat, undamaged examples.

Known Counterfeits: Collector counterfeits are not frequently encountered, but circulating counterfeits were struck in copper, lead, and white metal (tin and lead alloys), particularly during the 1850s-1860s.

Plain Obverse	VG	VF
1837	50.00	290.00

Plain Obverse	VG	VF
1838O	60.00	375.00

Stars On Obverse	VG	VF
1838, large stars	25.00	35.00
1839	25.00	35.00
1839O	30.00	40.00
1840	25.00	40.00
1840O	30.00	50.00
1840, extra drapery from elbow	50.00	185.00
1841	20.00	30.00
1841O	25.00	45.00
1842	18.00	25.00
1842O	25.00	75.00
1843	18.00	25.00
1843O	80.00	325.00
1844	350.00	800.00
1845	20.00	30.00
1845O	35.00	250.00
1846	350.00	950.00
1847	25.00	85.00
1848	20.00	50.00
1849	20.00	35.00
1849O	30.00	135.00
1850	20.00	35.00

1844 Seated Liberty Dime with Stars on Obverse

Stars On Obverse	VG	VF
1850O	25.00	90.00
1851	20.00	30.00
1851O	25.00	90.00
1852	15.00	25.00
1852O	30.00	125.00
1853, no arrows at date	125.00	295.00
1853, arrows at date	9.00	14.00
1853O, arrows at date	14.00	45.00
1854	9.00	15.00
1854O	11.00	25.00
1855	9.25	20.00
1856	18.00	25.00
1856O	20.00	35.00
1856S	225.00	550.00
1857	15.00	20.00
1857O	16.00	28.00
1858	15.00	20.00
1858O	25.00	85.00
1858S	200.00	475.00
1859	20.00	45.00
1859O	20.00	45.00
1859S	225.00	550.00
1860S	55.00	145.00

Legend On Obverse	VG	VF
1860	22.00	30.00
1860O	600.00	1,950.00
1861	17.00	23.00
1861S	90.00	275.00
1862	18.00	25.00
1862S	65.00	185.00
1863	500.00	900.00
1863S	55.00	145.00
1864	500.00	750.00
1864S	45.00	110.00
1865	575.00	875.00
1865S	55.00	145.00
1866	600.00	950.00
1866S	65.00	150.00
1867	700.00	1,100.00
1867S	60.00	150.00
1868	22.00	40.00
1868S	35.00	85.00
1869	35.00	80.00
1869S	30.00	55.00
1870	22.00	40.00
1870S	375.00	650.00
1871	20.00	33.00
1871CC	3,500.00	6,500.00

Legend On Obverse	VG	VF
1871S	55.00	130.00
1872	15.00	20.00
1872CC	1,250.00	3,000.00
1872S	65.00	150.00
1873, closed 3	15.00	22.00
1873, open 3	35.00	75.00
1873CC	—	April 1999 auction, $632,500
1873, arrows at date	20.00	55.00
1873CC, arrows at date	3,250.00	6,500.00
1873S, arrows at date	30.00	70.00
1874, arrows at date	18.00	50.00
1874CC, arrows at date	6,500.00	12,500.00
1874S, arrows at date	75.00	160.00
1875	16.00	20.00
1875CC	20.00	40.00
1875S	20.00	40.00
1876	20.00	25.00
1876CC	30.00	40.00
1876S	20.00	25.00
1877	20.00	25.00
1877CC	30.00	40.00
1877S	18.00	30.00

1877 Seated Liberty Dime with Legend on Obverse

Legend On Obverse	VG	VF
1878	15.00	20.00
1878CC	95.00	225.00
1879	310.00	425.00
1880	275.00	350.00
1881	300.00	400.00
1882	16.00	20.00
1883	16.00	20.00
1884	16.00	20.00
1884S	35.00	55.00
1885	16.00	20.00
1885S	650.00	1,750.00
1886	15.00	20.00
1886S	70.00	125.00
1887	16.00	20.00
1887S	15.00	20.00
1888	16.00	20.00
1888S	15.00	25.00
1889	16.00	20.00
1889S	18.00	45.00
1890	16.00	20.00
1890S	15.00	50.00
1891	16.00	20.00
18910	15.00	20.00
1891S	15.00	20.00

BARBER DIMES

The dime, quarter, and half dollar introduced in 1892 bear a portrait head of Liberty instead of an entire figure. They were designed by U.S. Mint Chief Engraver Charles E. Barber, after whom they have been popularly named. More practical than artistically adventurous, the design was considered rather boring if not unpleasant. Because of its small size, the Barber dime features a wreath design on its reverse rather than an eagle.

Known Counterfeits: The rare 1894S has been counterfeited.

	F	XF
1892	16.00	28.00
1892O	33.00	75.00
1892S	210.00	285.00
1893, 3 over 2	175.00	300.00
1893	20.00	45.00
1893O	135.00	190.00
1893S	40.00	85.00
1894	120.00	190.00
1894O	215.00	425.00
1894S, proof, rare	—	May 1996 auction, $451,000
1895	355.00	565.00

	F	XF
1895O	900.00	2,500.00
1895S	135.00	240.00
1896	55.00	100.00
1896O	300.00	465.00
1896S	310.00	385.00
1897	8.00	30.00
1897O	290.00	480.00
1897S	100.00	185.00
1898	7.50	30.00
1898O	90.00	200.00
1898S	35.00	80.00
1899	7.50	26.00
1899O	70.00	150.00
1899S	35.00	45.00
1900	7.00	25.00
1900O	115.00	225.00
1900S	13.00	30.00
1901	6.50	28.00
1901O	16.00	68.00
1901S	360.00	520.00
1902	5.50	23.00
1902O	15.00	63.00
1902S	60.00	135.00

1898S Barber Dime

	F	XF
1903	5.50	25.00
1903O	14.00	50.00
1903S	340.00	750.00
1904	6.25	25.00
1904S	160.00	335.00
1905	6.00	25.00
1905O	35.00	90.00
1905S	9.00	45.00
1906	3.75	22.00
1906D	7.00	35.00
1906O	50.00	100.00
1906S	13.00	45.00
1907	3.50	22.00
1907D	9.00	45.00
1907O	35.00	65.00
1907S	16.00	70.00
1908	3.50	22.00
1908D	5.00	30.00
1908O	45.00	90.00
1908S	12.00	45.00
1909	3.50	22.00
1909D	60.00	135.00

1903S Barber Dime

	F	XF
1909O	13.00	50.00
1909S	90.00	180.00
1910	3.25	22.00
1910D	8.50	50.00
1910S	50.00	110.00
1911	3.25	22.00
1911D	3.25	25.00
1911S	8.50	40.00
1912	3.25	22.00
1912D	3.25	22.00
1912S	6.00	35.00
1913	3.25	22.00
1913S	110.00	210.00
1914	3.25	22.00
1914D	3.25	22.00
1914S	8.00	40.00
1915	3.25	22.00
1915S	35.00	65.00
1916	3.25	22.00
1916S	4.25	25.00

MERCURY DIMES

The name Mercury for this dime is a misnomer. Designed by Adolph Weinman, it actually depicts Liberty wearing a winged cap, representing freedom of thought. It was received with wide acclaim for its artistic merit when it was first released as part of a program for the beautification of U.S. coinage. The reverse carries the ancient Roman fasces, a symbol of authority still seen in the U.S. Senate. The horizontal bands tying the fasces together do not always strike up distinctly from each other, and those coins with "fully split bands" often command a premium.

Known Counterfeits: These include 1916D, 1921, 1921D, 1931D, 1942/1, and 1942/1D, most of which have been made by altering the mintmark on a more common date. The 1923D is a fantasy; none was officially struck.

	VF	MS-60
1916	7.00	30.00
1916D	3,850.00	13,200.00
1916S	15.00	45.00
1917	5.50	30.00
1917D	25.00	120.00
1917S	6.50	65.00
1918	12.00	70.00
1918D	12.00	105.00

1916D Mercury Dime

	VF	MS-60
1918S	10.00	95.00
1919	5.50	37.00
1919D	25.00	180.00
1919S	17.00	180.00
1920	4.00	28.00
1920D	8.00	110.00
1920S	8.50	110.00
1921	265.00	1,150.00
1921D	365.00	1,250.00
1923	4.00	28.00
1923S	18.00	160.00
1924	4.50	42.00
1924D	22.00	175.00
1924S	12.00	170.00
1925	4.00	28.00
1925D	45.00	350.00
1925S	14.00	185.00
1926	3.00	25.00
1926D	10.00	125.00
1926S	70.00	865.00
1927	3.50	26.00
1927D	20.00	175.00
1927S	9.00	285.00
1928	3.50	28.00

1925D Mercury Dime

	VF	MS-60
1928D	20.00	175.00
1928S	6.50	125.00
1929	3.00	20.00
1929D	8.00	25.00
1929S	5.00	35.00
1930	3.75	26.00
1930S	6.50	80.00
1931	4.25	35.00
1931D	20.00	100.00
1931S	11.00	95.00
1934	3.00	30.00
1934D	7.50	50.00
1935	2.15	10.00
1935D	6.50	35.00
1935S	3.00	24.00
1936	2.50	9.00
1936D	4.25	30.00
1936S	3.00	20.00
1937	1.75	8.00
1937D	3.00	22.00
1937S	3.00	22.00
1938	1.75	13.00
1938D	5.00	18.00
1938S	3.25	20.00

1942/41 Mercury Dime

	VF	MS-60
1939	1.75	7.50
1939D	2.00	7.50
1939S	3.50	25.00
1940	1.50	6.00
1940D	1.75	8.00
1940S	1.75	8.50
1941	1.50	6.00
1941D	1.50	8.00
1941S	1.75	7.00
1942, 42 over 41	660.00	2,650.00
1942D, 42 over 41	825.00	2,700.00
1942	1.50	6.00
1942D	1.75	8.00
1942S	1.75	9.50
1943	1.50	6.00
1943D	1.75	7.75
1943S	1.75	9.00
1944	1.50	6.00
1944D	1.75	7.50
1944S	1.75	7.50
1945	1.50	6.00
1945D	1.75	6.50
1945S	1.50	7.00
1945S, micro S	9.00	30.00

ROOSEVELT DIMES

The dime was chosen to honor Franklin Roosevelt following his death because of his involvement in the March of Dimes. The president himself was crippled by polio.

U.S. Mint Chief Engraver John R. Sinnock designed the coin on a tight schedule. There are no true rarities in this series.

Known Counterfeits: Counterfeit Roosevelt dimes are quite rare.

Silver Composition	XF	MS-60
1946	1.50	2.00
1946D	1.50	2.25
1946S	1.50	2.35
1947	1.50	4.00
1947D	1.50	5.00
1947S	1.50	5.00
1948	1.50	4.50
1948D	2.00	6.00
1948S	1.75	5.00
1949	3.00	16.00
1949D	2.25	9.00
1949S	7.50	40.00
1950	2.25	10.00

Silver Composition	XF	MS-60
1950D	2.50	5.00
1950S	3.75	32.00

Silver Composition	AU	MS-60
1951	2.00	2.50
1951D	2.00	2.50
1951S	4.00	10.00
1952	2.00	2.50
1952D	2.00	2.50
1952S	2.75	5.50
1953	2.00	2.25
1953D	2.00	2.50
1953S	2.25	3.00
1954	2.00	2.25
1954D	2.00	2.25
1954S	2.00	2.25
1955	2.25	2.75
1955D	2.50	2.75
1955S	2.00	2.25
1956	2.00	2.25
1956D	2.00	2.25
1957	2.00	2.25
1957D	2.00	2.25
1958	2.00	2.25

1964 Roosevelt Dime

Silver Composition	AU	MS-60
1958D	2.00	2.25
1959	2.00	2.25
1959D	2.00	2.25
1960	2.00	2.25
1960D	2.00	2.25
1961	2.00	2.25
1961D	2.00	2.25
1962	2.00	2.25
1962D	2.00	2.25
1963	2.00	2.25
1963D	2.00	2.25
1964	2.00	2.25
1964D	2.00	2.25

Clad Composition	MS-65
1965	1.00
1966	1.00
1967	1.50
1968	1.00
1968D	1.00
1968S, proof	1.00
1969	3.00
1969D	1.00
1969S, proof	1.00

1968 Roosevelt Dime

Clad Composition	MS-65
1970	1.00
1970D	1.00
1970S, proof	.75
1971	2.00
1971D	1.00
1971S, proof	1.00
1972	1.00
1972D	1.00
1972S, proof	1.00
1973	1.00
1973D	1.00
1973S, proof	1.00
1974	1.00
1974D	1.00
1974S, proof	1.00
1975	1.00
1975D	1.00
1975S, proof	2.00
1976	1.50
1976D	1.00
1976S, proof	1.00
1977	1.00
1977D	1.00

Clad Composition	MS-65
1977S, proof	2.00
1978	1.00
1978D	1.00
1978S, proof	1.00
1979	1.00
1979D	1.00
1979, proof, type I	1.00
1979, proof, type II	2.00
1980P	1.00
1980D	.75
1980S, proof	1.00
1981P	1.00
1981D	1.00
1981S, proof	1.00
1982P	8.50
1982, no mintmark	300.00
1982D	3.00
1982S, proof	2.00
1983P	7.00
1983D	2.50
1983S, proof	2.00
1984P	1.00
1984D	2.00

Clad Composition	MS-65
1984S, proof	2.00
1985P	1.00
1985D	1.00
1985S, proof	1.00
1986P	2.00
1986D	2.00
1986S, proof	2.75
1987P	1.00
1987D	1.00
1987S, proof	1.00
1988P	1.00
1988D	1.00
1988S, proof	3.00
1989P	1.00
1989D	1.00
1989S, proof	4.00
1990P	1.00
1990D	1.00
1990S, proof	2.00
1991P	1.00
1991D	1.00
1991S, proof	3.00
1992P	1.00

Clad Composition	MS-65
1992D	1.00
1992S, proof	4.00
1992S, proof, silver	5.00
1993P	1.00
1993D	1.50
1993S, proof	7.00
1993S, proof, silver	9.00
1994P	1.00
1994D	1.00
1994S, proof	5.00
1994S, proof, sivler	9.00
1995	1.50
1995D	2.00
1995S, proof	20.00
1995S, proof, sivler	25.00
1996	1.00
1996D	1.00
1996W	25.00
1996S, proof	2.50
1996S, proof, silver	9.00
1997P	2.00
1997D	1.00
1997S, proof	11.00

Clad Composition	MS-65
1997S, proof, silver	25.00
1998P	1.00
1998D	1.25
1998S, proof	4.00
1998S, proof, silver	9.00
1999P	1.00
1999D	1.00
1999S, proof	4.00
1999S, proof, silver	6.50
2000P	1.00
2000D	1.00
2000S, proof	1.00
2000S, proof, silver	4.00
2001P	1.00
2001D	1.00
2001S, proof	3.00
2001S, proof, silver	5.00
2002P	1.00
2002D	1.00
2002S, proof	2.00
2002S, proof, silver	5.00
2003P	1.00
2003D	1.00

Clad Composition	MS-65
2003S, proof	2.00
2003S, proof, silver	4.00
2004P	1.00
2004D	1.00
2004S, proof	4.75
2004S, proof, silver	4.50
2005P	1.00
2005D	1.00
2005S, proof	2.25
2005S, proof, silver	3.50
2006P	1.00
2006D	1.00
2006S, proof	2.25
2006S, proof, silver	3.50
2007P	1.00
2007D	1.00
2007S, proof	2.25
2007S, proof, silver	3.50
2008P	1.00
2008D	1.00
2008S, proof	2.25
2008S, proof silver	3.50

TWENTY-CENT PIECES

When designing this coin, U.S. Mint officials were concerned about the public confusing it with a quarter. To give it a distinctive look, the eagle on the reverse faces its left rather than its right, as on the quarter; the word "Liberty" on the shield on the obverse is in relief rather than incuse; and the 20-cent coin's edge is plain rather than reeded.

The changes weren't enough, however, and the coin ceased circulation production after only two years. Only proofs for collectors were struck in 1877 and 1878.

Known Counterfeits: Mintmarks have been added to some authentic 1876 examples to make them appear to be 1876CC examples. Some 19th-century charlatans hand-scraped reeding into the edges of 20-cent coins in hopes of passing them off as quarters.

	VG	VF
1875	210.00	325.00
1875CC	385.00	600.00
1875S	110.00	175.00
1876	225.00	350.00
1876CC, rare	—	April 1997 auction, $148,500

	VG	VF
1877, proof	—	2,900.00
1878, proof	—	2,300.00

1876 Twenty-Cent Piece

SEATED LIBERTY QUARTERS

Following the introduction of Christian Gobrecht's Seated Liberty design on the silver dollar, smaller coins gradually adapted this design.

Several minor changes were implemented over the life of this coin. After the first few years, additional drapery was added below Liberty's elbow. The arrows by the date from 1853 to 1855 and the rays on the reverse in 1853 indicate a seven-percent reduction in weight. The arrows in 1873 to 1874 indicate a minuscule increase in weight. A ribbon with the motto "In God We Trust" was added over the eagle in 1866.

Known Counterfeits: Genuine 1858 quarters have been re-engraved to pass as 1853 no-arrows pieces. Contemporary counterfeits struck in copper, lead, and white metal (tin and lead alloys) exist.

	VG	VF
1838	50.00	110.00
1839	44.00	85.00
1840O	55.00	135.00
1840, extra drapery from elbow	55.00	125.00
1840O, extra drapery from elbow	40.00	115.00
1841	90.00	170.00

1847 Seated Liberty Quarter with No Motto Above Eagle

	VG	VF
1841O	30.00	85.00
1842	120.00	275.00
1842O, small date	650.00	1,950.00
1842O, large date	40.00	70.00
1843	25.00	45.00
1843O	30.00	125.00
1844	25.00	50.00
1844O	30.00	75.00
1845	25.00	45.00
1846	25.00	55.00
1847	25.00	50.00
1847O	45.00	135.00
1848	60.00	185.00
1849	30.00	65.00
1849O	750.00	1,850.00
1850	50.00	125.00
1850O	30.00	110.00
1851	75.00	225.00
1851O	275.00	700.00
1852	60.00	185.00
1852O	275.00	800.00
1853, no arrows at date	650.00	1,100.00

Arrows At Date	VG	VF
1853	25.00	45.00
1853, 3 over 4	65.50	200.00
1853O	35.00	100.00
1854	20.00	35.00
1854O	25.00	60.00
1854O, huge O	1,350.00	4,750.00
1855	20.00	35.00
1855O	75.00	240.00
1855S	60.00	225.00

No Arrows At Date	VG	VF
1856	20.00	35.00
1856O	30.00	60.00
1856S	65.00	250.00
1856S, S over S	275.00	1,250.00
1857	20.00	35.00
1857O	20.00	40.00
1857S	175.00	450.00
1858	20.00	35.00
1858O	30.00	70.00
1858S	110.00	300.00
1859	25.00	40.00
1859O	30.00	80.00

1853O Seated Liberty Quarter with
Arrrows at Date and Rays on Reverse

*1856 Seated Liberty Quarter
with Arrows Removed From Date*

No Arrows At Date	VG	VF
1859S	150.00	500.00
1860	20.00	30.00
1860O	30.00	55.00
1860S	350.00	975.00
1861	20.00	30.00
1861S	145.00	400.00
1862	20.00	40.00
1862S	125.00	325.00
1863	45.00	120.00
1864	120.00	245.00
1864S	600.00	1,350.00
1865	115.00	235.00
1865S	175.00	425.00

Motto Above Eagle	VG	VF
1866	600.00	1,000.00
1866S	375.00	1,050.00
1867	325.00	675.00
1867S	385.00	900.00
1868	250.00	400.00
1868S	110.00	300.00
1869	450.00	800.00
1869S	135.00	375.00
1870	80.00	245.00

1873 Seated Liberty Quarter, Open 3, with Motto Above Eagle

Motto Above Eagle	VG	VF
1870CC	6,500.00	15,000.00
1871	65.00	150.00
1871CC	4,500.00	12,500.00
1871S	500.00	950.00
1872	40.00	110.00
1872CC	1,500.00	3,750.00
1872S	1,250.00	2,400.00
1873, closed 3	350.00	800.00
1873, open 3	45.00	120.00
1873CC, six known	—	April 1999 auction, $106,375

Arrows At Date	VG	VF
1873	25.00	60.00
1873CC	4,500.00	11,000.00
1873S	40.00	140.00
1874	25.00	70.00
1874S	30.00	110.00

No Arrows At Date	VG	VF
1875	17.00	30.00
1875CC	110.00	350.00
1875S	35.00	110.00
1876	17.00	30.00
1876CC	40.00	65.00

1874S Seated Liberty Quarter with Arrows at Date

No Arrows At Date	VG	VF
1876S	20.00	30.00
1877	17.00	30.00
1877CC	40.00	65.00
1877S	17.00	30.00
1877S, over horizontal S	60.00	175.00
1878	18.00	35.00
1878CC	45.00	80.00
1878S	200.00	400.00
1879	235.00	325.00
1880	235.00	325.00
1881	250.00	350.00
1882	250.00	350.00
1883	265.00	365.00
1884	450.00	650.00
1885	265.00	365.00
1886	600.00	800.00
1887	350.00	550.00
1888	325.00	500.00
1888S	20.00	30.00
1889	300.00	425.00
1890	85.00	125.00
1891	20.00	30.00
1891O	225.00	550.00
1891S	20.00	65.00

1879 Seated Liberty Quarter with Arrows Removed From Date

BARBER QUARTERS

The quarter, dime, and half dollar introduced in 1892 bear a portrait head of Liberty instead of an entire figure. They were designed by U.S. Mint Chief Engraver Charles E. Barber, after whom they have been popularly named. More practical than artistically adventurous, the design was considered rather boring if not unpleasant. The reverses of the quarter and the half dollar have a fully spread heraldic eagle with a ribbon in its beak and a field of stars above. Barber quarters are common, and well-worn examples are often regarded as little more than bullion.

Known Counterfeits: 1913S suspected but not confirmed. Contemporary counterfeits in a tin-lead alloy are not rare.

	F	XF
1892	35.00	100.00
1892O	55.00	155.00
1892S	135.00	300.00
1893	25.00	70.00
1893O	45.00	165.00
1893S	80.00	255.00
1894	35.00	95.00

1892 Barber Quarter

	F	XF
1894O	50.00	165.00
1894S	38.00	115.00
1895	32.00	80.00
1895O	46.00	135.00
1895S	45.00	110.00
1896	25.00	80.00
1896O	115.00	425.00
1896S	1,800.00	4,300.00
1897	22.00	75.00
1897O	115.00	395.00
1897S	275.00	440.00
1898	23.00	75.00
1898O	75.00	295.00
1898S	48.00	96.00
1899	23.00	75.00
1899O	35.00	130.00
1899S	70.00	135.00
1900	22.00	72.00
1900O	63.00	150.00
1900S	38.00	80.00
1901	25.00	80.00
1901O	145.00	455.00
1901S	17,500.00	30,000.00

	F	XF
1902	20.00	65.00
1902O	50.00	150.00
1902S	55.00	170.00
1903	20.00	60.00
1903O	40.00	125.00
1903S	45.00	145.00
1904	20.00	70.00
1904O	60.00	225.00
1905	25.00	70.00
1905O	80.00	265.00
1905S	45.00	110.00
1906	18.50	65.00
1906D	25.00	70.00
1906O	40.00	110.00
1907	16.50	60.00
1907D	30.00	80.00
1907O	19.00	65.00
1907S	50.00	135.00
1908	18.50	65.00
1908D	17.50	65.00
1908O	17.50	70.00
1908S	90.00	295.00
1909	17.50	65.00

	F	XF
1909D	20.00	90.00
1909O	95.00	375.00
1909S	35.00	95.00
1910	30.00	80.00
1910D	45.00	130.00
1911	20.00	70.00
1911D	95.00	330.00
1911S	50.00	180.00
1912	17.50	70.00
1912S	45.00	130.00
1913	75.00	390.00
1913D	40.00	95.00
1913S	5,000.00	10,500.00
1914	17.00	55.00
1914D	17.00	55.00
1914S	235.00	620.00
1915	17.00	55.00
1915D	17.00	55.00
1915S	35.00	110.00
1916	17.00	55.00
1916D	17.00	55.00

1903 Barber Quarter

STANDING LIBERTY QUARTERS

Hermon MacNeil's Standing Liberty quarter design originally depicted Liberty with her right breast exposed ("type I"). Some members of the public took offense at the time, but many prominent artists thought it was an excellent example of inspired neo-classical art. The design was modified in its second year of production to cover Liberty's breast ("type II").

Similar to the Buffalo nickel, the date's original high relief caused the numerals to wear quickly. This was partially remedied in 1925 by carving out the date area and placing the numerals in recess. There were also problems with Liberty's head not striking up fully. As a result, high-grade pieces with Liberty's head fully struck command premiums. Examples with the date worn off are worth only bullion value.

Known Counterfeits: 1916 altered from 1917, 1917 Type I, 1918/7S, 1923S (altered, including all with round-topped 3), 1927S (altered).

	F	XF
1916, type I	9,500.00	14,500.00
1917, type I	50.00	95.00
1917D, type I	55.00	125.00
1917S, type I	60.00	160.00

1916 Standing Liberty Quarter

	F	XF
1917, type II	40.00	75.00
1917D, type II	65.00	110.00
1917S	65.00	110.00
1918	30.00	45.00
1918D	65.00	120.00
1918S	30.00	50.00
1918S, 8 over 7	3,850.00	7,500.00
1919	55.00	80.00
1919D	195.00	565.00
1919S	185.00	510.00
1920	25.00	50.00
1920D	90.00	160.00
1920S	30.00	60.00
1921	450.00	750.00
1923	35.00	55.00
1923S	675.00	1,250.00
1924	25.00	45.00

	F	XF
1924D	110.00	185.00
1924S	45.00	105.00
1925	7.00	45.00
1926	6.00	35.00
1926D	20.00	75.00
1926S	11.00	110.00
1927	6.00	30.00
1927D	30.00	140.00
1927S	110.00	1,000.00
1928	6.00	30.00
1928D	7.50	40.00
1928S	10.00	65.00
1929	6.00	30.00
1929D	6.75	35.00
1929S	6.50	35.00
1930	6.00	30.00
1930S	6.50	35.00

1927S Standing Liberty Quarter

WASHINGTON QUARTERS

The Washington quarter was intended to be a one year commemorative for the 200th anniversary of Washington's birth. Its release was delayed because of the U.S. Treasury's decision to change designers from Laura Gardin Fraser to John Flanagan. Both designs were based on Jean Antoine Houdon's 1785 bust of Washington. Eventually it was decided to replace the Standing Liberty quarter with the Washington design, which enjoyed immense initial popularity.

Several dates in the 1930s are characterized by weak rims, making grading difficult. Quarters dated 1934 and 1935 do not have this problem. The 1964 pieces were aggressively hoarded in uncirculated rolls, and as such are common today. A special reverse was used in 1975 and 1976 (all dated "1776-1976") to commemorate the U.S. Bicentennial. It depicts the bust of a Colonial drummer designed by Jack L. Ahr.

Known Counterfeits: 1932D and 1932S quarters with false mintmarks exist. Counterfeits of high-grade 1932 and 1934 pieces also exist.

Silver Composition	VF	MS-60
1932	7.50	25.00
1932D	240.00	1,000.00
1932S	240.00	500.00
1934	5.50	30.00
1934D	13.50	245.00
1935	5.00	20.00
1935D	14.00	255.00
1935S	7.50	100.00
1936	5.00	20.00
1936D	20.00	625.00
1936S	6.25	115.00
1937	5.00	25.00
1937D	6.25	65.00
1937S	15.00	170.00
1938	6.25	95.00
1938S	9.75	110.00
1939	5.00	16.00
1939D	5.25	45.00
1939S	9.00	110.00
1940	5.00	18.50
1940D	13.00	135.00

1936D Washington Quarter

Silver Composition	VF	MS-60
1940S	6.50	30.00
1941	2.00	9.75
1941D	3.50	35.00
1941S	3.50	30.00
1942	2.00	5.50
1942D	3.50	20.00
1942S	3.75	80.00
1943	2.00	5.00
1943D	3.75	30.00
1943S	5.00	30.00
1944	2.00	5.00
1944D	3.50	20.00
1944S	3.50	15.00
1945	1.75	5.00
1945D	3.50	20.00
1945S	3.50	9.00
1946	2.00	5.00
1946D	3.50	10.00
1946S	3.50	9.00
1947	2.25	11.50
1947D	3.50	11.00
1947S	3.50	10.00
1948	3.50	5.50

1945 Washington Quarter

Silver Composition	VF	MS-60
1948D	3.50	13.50
1948S	3.50	8.00
1949	3.50	40.00
1949D	3.50	18.00
1950	2.00	5.50
1950D	2.00	5.00
1950D, D over S	60.00	275.00
1950S	2.00	9.00
1950S, S over D	70.00	400.00
1951	2.00	6.00
1951D	2.00	7.00
1951S	4.50	25.00
1952	2.00	5.50
1952D	2.00	5.00
1952S	4.00	20.00
1953	2.00	5.50
1953D	1.75	4.25
1953S	2.00	5.00
1954	2.00	5.00
1954D	1.75	4.75
1954S	1.75	4.00
1955	1.50	3.50
1955D	2.50	6.50

1953D Washington Quarter

Silver Composition	VF	MS-60
1956	1.75	4.00
1956D	2.00	5.00
1957	—	3.50
1957D	—	3.50
1958	—	4.50
1958D	—	4.50
1959	—	4.50
1959D	—	4.50
1960	—	4.50
1960D	—	4.50
1961	—	4.50
1961D	—	4.50
1962	—	4.50
1962D	—	4.50
1963	—	4.50
1963D	—	4.50
1964	—	4.50
1964D	—	4.50

Clad Composition	MS-60
1965	.75
1966	.85
1967	.85
1968	1.00

1966 Washington Quarter

Clad Composition	MS-60
1968D	1.00
1968S, proof	1.50
1969	1.50
1969D	1.75
1969S, proof	.70
1970	.60
1970D	.60
1970S, proof	1.50
1971	.60
1971D	.60
1971S, proof	.75
1972	.60
1972D	.60
1972S, proof	.75
1973	.60
1973D	.60
1973S, proof	.70
1974	.70
1974D	.60
1974S, proof	.85
1976, Bicentennial	.60
1976D, Bicentennial	.60
1976S, Bicentennial, proof	.75

Clad Composition	MS-60
1976S, Bicentennial, silver clad	2.00
1977	.50
1977D	.50
1977S, proof	.75
1978	.75
1978D	.85
1978S, proof	.75
1979	.75
1979D	.65
1979S, proof, type I	.75
1979S, proof, type II	1.00
1980P	.60
1980D	.60
1980S, proof	1.00
1981P	1.00
1981D	1.00
1981S, proof	1.25
1982P	4.50
1982D	3.50
1982S, proof	1.00
1983P	12.50
1983D	9.00
1983S, proof	1.50

Clad Composition	MS-60
1984P	1.50
1984D	1.25
1984S, proof	1.50
1985P	2.50
1985D	1.00
1985S, proof	1.00
1986P	1.50
1986D	4.00
1986S, proof	1.25
1987P	.65
1987D	.50
1987S, proof	.75
1988P	1.00
1988D	.75
1988S, proof	1.00
1989P	.85
1989D	.60
1989S, proof	1.00
1990P	.50
1990D	.50
1990S, proof	3.00
1991P	.75
1991D	.60

Clad Composition	MS-60
1991S, proof	1.25
1992P	.60
1992D	.75
1992S, proof	1.50
1992S, proof, silver	2.25
1993P	.60
1993D	1.00
1993S, proof	2.50
1993S, proof, silver	3.50
1994P	.60
1994D	.50
1994S, proof	1.50
1994S, proof, silver	7.50
1995P	1.00
1995D	.60
1995S, proof	7.00
1995S, proof, silver	7.50
1996P	.50
1996D	.50
1996S, proof	2.50
1996S, proof, silver	10.00
1997P	.50
1997D	.50

Clad Composition	MS-60
1997S, proof	5.00
1997S, proof, silver	12.00
1998P	.50
1998D	.50
1998S, proof	6.00
1998S, proof, silver	6.00

STATE QUARTERS

In 1992, to commemorate its 125th anniversary, Canada released a set of circulating commemorative quarters honoring each province and territory. The series became quite popular. Partially inspired by this Canadian series, the United States authorized a set of quarters honoring the 50 states. Congress wanted to "promote the diffusion of knowledge among the youth of the United States about the individual states, their history and geography, and the rich diversity of the national heritage."

Five were released each year from 1999 to 2008 in the order the states ratified the Constitution or joined the Union. In addition to the circulation strikes, proof examples in clad and traditional silver compositions were issued.

Although the 50 State Quarters program was completed in 2008, collectors can watch for six more special quarters dated 2009. The 2009 issues honor the District of Columbia and the five U.S. territories: the Commonwealth of Puerto Rico, Guam, American Samoa, the U.S. Virgin Islands, and the Commonwealth of the Northern Mariana Islands.

The coins were scheduled to be released in 2009 in the order listed above. Like the 50 State Quarters, the obverses carry the traditional image of Washington and the reverses carry designs emblematic of the district or respective territory. The design selection process was similar to the process for the state quarters.

Also like the 50 State Quarters, the U.S. Mint was scheduled to strike and sell special collector versions for inclusion in mint and proof sets, and in the 90-percent-silver composition.

Known Counterfeits: Apparently risqué designs are actually satirical tokens struck with privately made dies on real quarters.

2009 District of Columbia Quarter

2009 Puerto Rico Quarter

2009 Guam Quarter

2009 American Samoa Quarter

2009 U.S. Virgin Islands Quarter

2009 Northern Mariana Islands Quarter

	MS-63	PF-65
1999P Delaware	1.50	—
1999D Delaware	1.25	—
1999S Delaware, proof	—	12.00
1999S Delaware, proof, silver	—	65.00
1999P Pennsylvania	1.00	—
1999D Pennsylvania	1.00	—
1999S Pennsylvania, proof	—	12.00
1999S Pennsylvania, proof, silver	—	65.00
1999P New Jersey	1.00	—
1999D New Jersey	1.00	—
1999S New Jersey, proof	—	12.00
1999S New Jersey, proof, silver	—	65.00
1999P Georgia	1.25	—
1999D Georgia	1.25	—
1999S Georgia, proof	—	12.00
1999S Georgia, proof, silver	—	65.00
1999P Connecticut	1.00	—
1999D Connecticut	1.00	—
1999S Connecticut, proof	—	12.00
1999S Connecticut, proof, silver	—	65.00

Delaware (1999)

Pennsylvania (1999)

New Jersey (1999)

Georgia (1999)

Connecticut (1999)

	MS-63	PF-65
2000P Massachusetts	1.00	—
2000D Massachusetts	1.00	—
2000S Massachusetts, proof	—	3.50
2000S Massachusetts, proof, silver	—	5.50
2000P Maryland	1.00	—
2000D Maryland	1.00	—
2000S Maryland, proof	—	3.50
2000S Maryland, proof, silver	—	5.50
2000P South Carolina	1.50	—
2000D South Carolina	1.50	—
2000S South Carolina, proof	—	3.50
2000S South Carolina, proof, silver	—	5.50
2000P New Hampshire	1.00	—
2000D New Hampshire	1.00	—
2000S New Hampshire, proof	—	3.50
2000S New Hampshire, proof, silver	—	5.50
2000P Virginia	1.00	—
2000D Virginia	1.00	—
2000S Virginia, proof	—	3.50
2000S Virginia, proof, silver	—	5.50

Massachusetts
(2000)

Maryland (2000)

South Carolina
(2000)

New Hampshire (2000)

Virginia (2000)

	MS-63	PF-65
2001P New York	1.00	—
2001D NewYork	1.00	—
2001S New York, proof	—	11.00
2001S New York, proof, silver	—	25.00
2001P North Carolina	1.00	—
2001D North Carolina	1.00	—
2001S North Carolina, proof	—	11.00
2001S North Carolina, proof, silver	—	22.00
2001P Rhode Island	1.00	—
2001D Rhode Island	1.00	—
2001S Rhode Island, proof	—	11.00
2001S Rhode Island, proof, silver	—	20.00
2001P Vermont	1.25	—
2001D Vermont	1.00	—
2001S Vermont, proof	—	11.00
2001S Vermont, proof, silver	—	20.00
2001P Kentucky	1.25	—
2001D Kentucky	1.00	—
2001S Kentucky, proof	—	11.00
2001S Kentucky, proof, silver	—	20.00

New York (2001)

North Carolina (2001)

Rhode Island (2001)

Vermont (2001)

Kentucky (2001)

	MS-63	PF-65
2002P Tennessee	1.50	—
2002D Tennessee	1.50	—
2002S Tennessee, proof	—	4.00
2002S Tennessee, proof, silver	—	9.00
2002P Ohio	1.00	—
2002D Ohio	1.00	—
2002S Ohio, proof	—	4.00
2002S Ohio, proof, silver	—	9.00
2002P Louisiana	1.00	—
2002D Louisiana	1.00	—
2002S Louisiana, proof	—	4.00
2002S Louisiana, proof, silver	—	9.00
2002P Indiana	1.00	—
2002D Indiana	1.00	—
2002S Indiana, proof	—	4.00
2002S Indiana, proof, silver	—	9.00
2002P Mississippi	1.00	—
2002D Mississippi	1.00	—
2002S Mississippi, proof	—	4.00
2002S Mississippi, proof, silver	—	9.00

Tennessee (2002)

Ohio (2002)

Louisiana (2002)

Indiana (2002)

Mississippi (2002)

	MS-63	PF-65
2003P Illinois	1.00	—
2003D Illinois	1.00	—
2003S Illinois, proof	—	3.50
2003S Illinois, proof, silver	—	5.25
2003P Alabama	1.00	—
2003D Alabama	1.00	—
2003S Alabama, proof	—	3.50
2003S Alabama, proof, silver	—	5.25
2003P Maine	1.00	—
2003D Maine	1.00	—
2003S Maine, proof	—	3.50
2003S Maine, proof, silver	—	5.25
2003P Missouri	1.00	—
2003D Missouri	1.00	—
2003S Missouri, proof	—	3.50
2003S Missouri, proof, silver	—	5.25
2003P Arkansas	1.00	—
2003D Arkansas	1.00	—
2003S Arkansas, proof	—	3.50
2003S Arkansas, proof, silver	—	5.25

Illinois (2003)

Alabama (2003)

Maine (2003)

Missouri (2003)

Arkansas (2003)

	MS-63	PF-65
2004P Michigan	.75	—
2004D Michigan	.75	—
2004S Michigan, proof	—	5.00
2004S Michigan, proof, silver	—	6.00
2004P Florida	.75	—
2004D Florida	.75	—
2004S Florida, proof	—	5.00
2004S Florida, proof, silver	—	6.00
2004P Texas	.75	—
2004D Texas	.75	—
2004S Texas, proof	—	5.00
2004S Texas, proof, silver	—	6.00
2004P Iowa	.75	—
2004D Iowa	.75	—
2004S Iowa, proof	—	5.00
2004S Iowa, proof, silver	—	6.00
2004P Wisconsin	1.00	—
2004D Wisconsin	1.00	—
2004S Wisconsin, proof	—	5.00
2004S Wisconsin, proof, silver	—	6.00

Michigan (2004)

Florida (2004)

Texas (2004)

Iowa (2004)

Wisconsin (2004)

	MS-63	PF-65
2005P California	.75	—
2005D California	.75	—
2005S California, proof	—	3.00
2005S California, proof, silver	—	5.50
2005P Minnesota	.75	—
2005D Minnesota	.75	—
2005S Minnesota, proof	—	3.00
2005S Minnesota, proof, silver	—	5.50
2005P Oregon	.75	—
2005D Oregon	.75	—
2005S Oregon, proof	—	3.00
2005S Oregon, proof, silver	—	5.50
2005P Kansas	.75	—
2005D Kansas	.75	—
2005S Kansas, proof	—	3.00
2005S Kansas, proof, silver	—	5.50
2005P West Virginia	.75	—
2005D West Virginia	.75	—
2005S West Virginia, proof	—	3.00
2005S West Virginia, proof, silver	—	5.50

California (2005)

Minnesota (2005)

Oregon (2005)

Kansas (2005)

West Virginia (2005)

	MS-63	PF-65
2006P Nevada	.75	—
2006D Nevada	.75	—
2006S Nevada, proof	—	5.00
2006S Nevada, proof, silver	—	5.75
2006P Nebraska	.75	—
2006D Nebraska	.75	—
2006S Nebraska, proof	—	5.00
2006S Nebraska, proof, silver	—	5.75
2006P Colorado	.75	—
2006D Colorado	.75	—
2006S Colorado, proof	—	5.00
2006S Colorado, proof, silver	—	5.75
2006P North Dakota	.75	—
2006D North Dakota	.75	—
2006S North Dakota, proof	—	5.00
2006S North Dakota, proof, silver	—	5.75
2006P South Dakota	.75	—
2006D South Dakota	.75	—
2006S South Dakota, proof	—	5.00
2006S South Dakota, proof, silver	—	5.75

Nevada (2006)

Nebraska (2006)

Colorado (2006)

North Dakota (2006)

South Dakota (2006)

	MS-63	PF-65
2007P Montana	.75	—
2007D Montana	.75	—
2007S Montana, proof	—	4.00
2007S Montana, proof, silver	—	6.50
2007P Washington	.75	—
2007D Washington	.75	—
2007S Washington, proof	—	4.00
2007S Washington, proof, silver	—	6.50
2007P Idaho	.75	—
2007D Idaho	.75	—
2007S Idaho, proof	—	4.00
2007S Idaho, proof, silver	—	6.50
2007P Wyoming	.75	—
2007D Wyoming	.75	—
2007S Wyoming, proof	—	4.00
2007S Wyoming, proof, silver	—	6.50
2007P Utah	.75	—
2007D Utah	.75	—
2007S Utah, proof	—	4.00
2007S Utah, proof, silver	—	6.50

Montana (2007)

Washington (2007)

Idaho (2007)

Wyoming (2007)

Utah (2007)

	MS-63	PF-65
2008P Oklahoma	.75	—
2008D Oklahoma	.75	—
2008S Oklahoma, proof	—	4.00
2008S Oklahoma, silver, proof	—	6.50
2008P New Mexico	.75	—
2008D New Mexico	.75	—
2008S New Mexico, proof	—	4.00
2008S New Mexico, silver, proof	—	6.50
2008P Arizona	.75	—
2008D Arizona	.75	—
2008S Arizona, proof	—	4.00
2008S Arizona, silver, proof	—	6.50
2008P Alaska	.75	—
2008D Alaska	.75	—
2008S Alaska, proof	—	4.00
2008S Alaska, silver, proof	—	6.50
2008P Hawaii	.75	—
2008D Hawaii	.75	—
2008S Hawaii, proof	—	4.00
2008S Hawaii, silver, proof	—	6.50

Oklahoma (2008)

New Mexico (2008)

Arizona (2008)

Alaska (2008)

Hawaii (2008)

SEATED LIBERTY HALF DOLLARS

Following the introduction of Christian Gobrecht's Seated Liberty design on the silver dollar, smaller coins gradually adapted this design.

Several minor changes were made over the coin's life. During its first year, drapery was added below Liberty's elbow. The arrows by the date from 1853 to 1855 and the rays on the reverse in 1853 indicate a seven-percent reduction in weight. Arrows at the date in 1873 and 1874 indicate a minuscule increase in weight. Most of the 1861O pieces were struck after Louisiana seceded from the Union. A ribbon with the motto "In God We Trust" was added over the eagle in 1866. Seated Liberty half dollars are often found cleaned. Watch for retoned specimens.

Known Counterfeits: Genuine 1858O half dollars have been re-engraved to pass as 1853O no-arrows pieces. Some with-arrows pieces have had the arrows removed for the same reason. Contemporary counterfeits struck in tin and lead alloys are often found.

	VG	VF
1839, no drapery below elbow	110.00	340.00
1839, with drapery	55.00	85.00

1839 Seated Liberty Half Dollar with
No Motto Above Eagle and No Drapery Below Elbow

	VG	VF
1840, small letters on reverse	45.00	85.00
1840, reverse of 1838	200.00	350.00
1840O	50.00	90.00
1841	65.00	150.00
1841O	45.00	80.00
1842, small date	55.00	120.00
1842, large date	40.00	65.00
1842O, small date	850.00	2,450.00
1842O, large date	40.00	90.00
1843	40.00	65.00
1843O	40.00	65.00
1844	40.00	60.00
1844O	40.00	70.00
1844O, over 1844	775.00	1,300.00
1845	45.00	125.00
1845O	40.00	70.00
1845O, no drapery	50.00	115.00
1846	40.00	70.00
1846, 6 over horizontal 6	250.00	450.00
1846O, medium-size date	40.00	65.00
1846O, tall date	285.00	620.00
1847, 7 over 6	2,750.00	5,250.00
1847	45.00	70.00

	VG	VF
1847O	40.00	65.00
1848	65.00	185.00
1848O	40.00	70.00
1849	45.00	70.00
1849O	40.00	70.00
1850	325.00	550.00
1850O	30.00	80.00
1851	450.00	850.00
1851O	55.00	120.00
1852	500.00	925.00
1852O	125.00	350.00
1853O, no arrows at date, rare	154,000.00	—

Arrows At Date, Rays On Reverse	VG	VF
1853	35.00	90.00
1853O	50.00	125.00

Arrows At Date, No Rays	VG	VF
1854	40.00	60.00
1854O	40.00	60.00
1855, 5 over 4	85.00	250.00
1855	40.00	65.00
1855O	40.00	60.00
1855S	475.00	1,500.00

1853 Seated Liberty Half Dollar
with Arrows at Date and Rays on Reverse

*1854 Seated Liberty Half Dollar
with Arrows at Date, No Rays on Reverse*

No Arrows At Date	VG	VF
1856	40.00	70.00
1856O	40.00	60.00
1856S	120.00	260.00
1857	40.00	60.00
1857O	40.00	85.00
1857S	120.00	285.00
1858	40.00	60.00
1858O	40.00	60.00
1858S	50.00	110.00
1859	40.00	70.00
1859O	40.00	60.00
1859S	45.00	100.00
1860	40.00	100.00
1860O	40.00	70.00
1860S	40.00	85.00
1861	40.00	65.00
1861O	40.00	85.00
1861S	45.00	70.00
1862	50.00	120.00
1862S	40.00	75.00
1863	50.00	85.00
1863S	45.00	70.00

1858S Seated Liberty Half Dollar
with Arrows Removed From Date

No Arrows At Date	VG	VF
1864	50.00	120.00
1864S	45.00	70.00
1865	45.00	90.00
1865S	45.00	70.00
1866, proof, unique	—	—
1866S	575.00	1,250.00

Motto Above Eagle	VG	VF
1866	45.00	80.00
1866S	45.00	70.00
1867	50.00	110.00
1867S	40.00	70.00
1868	55.00	185.00
1868S	40.00	70.00
1869	45.00	70.00
1869S	45.00	70.00
1870	45.00	80.00
1870CC	1,500.00	3,900.00
1870S	45.00	85.00
1871	40.00	75.00
1871CC	325.00	1,200.00
1871S	40.00	70.00
1872	40.00	75.00
1872CC	125.00	400.00

1872CC Seated Liberty Half Dollar with Motto Above Eagle

Motto Above Eagle	VG	VF
1872S	45.00	135.00
1873, closed 3	45.00	100.00
1873, open 3	3,400.00	5,500.00
1873CC	320.00	950.00
1873S, no arrows at date, none known	—	—

Arrows At Date	VG	VF
1873	50.00	90.00
1873CC	275.00	850.00
1873S	80.00	245.00
1874	40.00	85.00
1874CC	575.00	1,750.00
1874S	65.00	185.00

No Arrows At Date	VG	VF
1875	40.00	55.00
1875CC	55.00	125.00
1875S	40.00	65.00
1876	40.00	55.00
1876CC	55.00	115.00
1876S	40.00	55.00
1877	40.00	55.00
1877CC	55.00	115.00

1873 Seated Liberty Half Dollar with Arrows at Date

No Arrows At Date	VG	VF
1877S	40.00	55.00
1878	45.00	80.00
1878CC	600.00	1,500.00
1878S	37,500.00	47,500.00
1879	310.00	400.00
1880	280.00	355.00
1881	300.00	385.00
1882	365.00	450.00
1883	340.00	435.00
1884	375.00	500.00
1885	425.00	550.00
1886	500.00	700.00
1887	525.00	775.00
1888	300.00	400.00
1889	315.00	400.00
1890	310.00	415.00
1891	60.00	120.00

1878S Seated Liberty Half Dollar
with Arrows Removed From Date

BARBER HALF DOLLARS

The half dollar, quarter, and dime introduced in 1892 bear a portrait of Liberty's head instead of an entire figure. They were designed by U.S. Mint Chief Engraver Charles E. Barber, after whom they have been popularly named. More practical than artistically adventurous, the design was considered rather boring if not unpleasant. The reverses of the half dollar and quarter have a fully spread heraldic eagle with a ribbon in its beak and a field of stars above. This new design for the half dollar came only a year following its resurrection as an actively minted denomination.

Barbers are common, and well-worn examples are often regarded as little more than silver bullion. Strong middle grades, on the other hand, are surprisingly difficult to obtain.

Known Counterfeits: Contemporary counterfeits in a tin-lead alloy are common. Altered 1913, 1914, and 1915 coins with mintmarks removed are known.

	VG	VF
1892	40.00	120.00
1892O	420.00	575.00
1892S	330.00	530.00
1893	35.00	135.00

1892 Barber Half Dollar

	VG	VF
1893O	65.00	220.00
1893S	225.00	500.00
1894	50.00	200.00
1894O	35.00	170.00
1894S	30.00	125.00
1895	25.00	150.00
1895O	40.00	195.00
1895S	55.00	235.00
1896	30.00	160.00
1896O	55.00	290.00
1896S	145.00	350.00
1897	15.00	100.00
1897O	230.00	835.00
1897S	225.00	535.00
1898	16.00	95.00
1898O	75.00	355.00
1898S	50.00	175.00
1899	16.00	100.00
1899O	35.00	170.00
1899S	40.00	135.00
1900	16.00	90.00
1900O	20.00	165.00
1900S	20.00	100.00

	VG	VF
1901	16.00	95.00
1901O	25.00	205.00
1901S	55.00	355.00
1902	14.00	85.00
1902O	17.00	105.00
1902S	19.00	150.00
1903	16.00	100.00
1903O	17.00	115.00
1903S	18.00	125.00
1904	14.00	85.00
1904O	30.00	220.00
1904S	70.00	550.00
1905	30.00	180.00
1905O	45.00	235.00
1905S	18.00	125.00
1906	15.00	85.00
1906D	14.00	90.00
1906O	14.00	100.00
1906S	16.00	110.00
1907	14.00	85.00
1907D	14.00	75.00
1907O	14.00	90.00
1907S	20.00	165.00

1903 Barber Half Dollar

	VG	VF
1908	14.00	80.00
1908D	14.00	80.00
1908O	14.00	90.00
1908S	25.00	160.00
1909	16.00	85.00
1909O	25.00	140.00
1909S	14.00	100.00
1910	25.00	170.00
1910S	17.00	100.00
1911	14.00	85.00
1911D	16.00	90.00
1911S	17.00	100.00
1912	14.00	85.00
1912D	14.00	80.00
1912S	20.00	100.00
1913	90.00	420.00
1913D	20.00	100.00
1913S	25.00	110.00
1914	175.00	550.00
1914S	19.00	100.00
1915	170.00	380.00
1915D	14.00	75.00
1915S	20.00	95.00

19080 Barber Half Dollar

WALKING LIBERTY HALF DOLLARS

This beautiful half dollar was designed by Adolph Weinman, the designer of the Mercury dime, released in the same year. It depicts Liberty—the American flag draped about her and flowing in the breeze—progressing toward the dawn of a new day. It was received with wide acclaim for its artistic merit when it was released as part of a program to beautify U.S. coinage. The reverse carries an eagle perched on a rocky crag. The obverse design proved so popular that it was resurrected in 1986 for use on the new silver American Eagle bullion coins. Originally the mintmarks on this coin appeared on the obverse, but they were moved to the reverse in 1917.

Liberty's head did not always strike up fully. High-grade examples with Liberty's head fully struck are worth more.

Known Counterfeits: 1916S and 1938D coins with mintmarks added are known. All 1928D half dollars are all counterfeit.

	F	XF
1916	100.00	250.00
1916D	80.00	225.00
1916S	285.00	650.00
1917	9.00	45.00
1917D, obverse mintmark	80.00	235.00

	F	XF
1917D, reverse mintmark	45.00	275.00
1917S, obverse mintmark	135.00	720.00
1917S, reverse mintmark	17.00	65.00
1918	16.00	160.00
1918D	35.00	235.00
1918S	15.00	65.00
1919	80.00	550.00
1919D	100.00	765.00
1919S	75.00	850.00
1920	16.00	75.00
1920D	70.00	475.00
1920S	20.00	235.00
1921	350.00	1,550.00
1921D	550.00	2,200.00
1921S	220.00	4,800.00
1923S	28.00	315.00
1927S	14.00	160.00
1928S	15.00	200.00
1929D	19.00	110.00
1929S	13.00	115.00
1933S	13.00	60.00
1934	5.25	11.00
1934D	5.75	30.00

1921D Walking Liberty Half Dollar

	F	XF
1934S	5.75	25.00
1935	5.50	9.00
1935D	5.75	30.00
1935S	5.75	30.00
1936	5.25	8.50
1936D	5.75	20.00
1936S	5.75	20.00
1937	5.25	8.50
1937D	8.50	35.00
1937S	5.75	25.00
1938	5.75	9.50
1938D	115.00	220.00
1939	6.50	8.50
1939D	5.25	8.50
1939S	5.75	25.00
1940	7.00	9.00
1940S	5.25	12.00
1941	5.00	9.00
1941D	5.25	10.00
1941S	5.25	12.00
1942	5.00	9.00
1942D	5.25	10.00

1944 Walking Liberty Half Dollar

	F	XF
1942D, D over S	42.00	80.00
1942S	5.25	10.00
1943	7.00	9.00
1943D	5.25	10.00
1943S	5.25	10.00
1944	7.00	9.00
1944D	5.25	10.00
1944S	5.25	10.00
1945	7.00	9.00
1945D	5.25	10.00
1945S	5.25	10.00
1946	5.00	9.00
1946D	5.25	25.00
1946S	5.25	12.00
1947	7.50	11.00
1947D	5.25	14.00

FRANKLIN HALF DOLLARS

Similar to the Washington quarter, the Franklin half-dollar design was used in opposition from the Commission of Fine Arts. The reverse depicts the Liberty Bell as its prime motif, despite a law requiring all coins larger than a dime to bear an eagle. That is why a small eagle was added at the side of the bell as an afterthought. The coin was designed by U.S. Mint Chief Engraver John R. Sinnock, but the small eagle was engraved by a young Frank Gasparro, who later became chief engraver.

The horizontal lines on the Liberty Bell posed the biggest problem when striking the coin. Mint-state examples with fully struck bell lines often sell for significantly more.

Known Counterfeits: It is possible that none exist.

	XF	MS-60
1948	8.50	15.00
1948D	8.00	15.00
1949	6.25	40.00
1949D	7.25	45.00
1949S	11.00	60.00
1950	4.50	25.00
1950D	5.50	20.00
1951	4.75	11.00
1951D	8.50	25.00
1951S	5.25	20.00
1952	4.25	5.25
1952D	4.25	5.25
1952S	15.00	50.00
1953	10.00	25.00

1953 Franklin Half Dollar

	XF	MS-60
1953D	4.25	15.00
1953S	5.25	25.00
1954	4.25	5.25
1954D	4.25	5.25
1954S	5.00	14.00
1955	19.00	22.00
1955, "Bugs Bunny" teeth	25.00	28.00
1956	4.75	13.50
1957	4.25	5.25
1957D	4.25	5.25
1958	4.25	5.25
1958D	4.25	5.25
1959	4.25	5.25
1959D	4.25	5.25
1960	4.25	5.25
1960D	4.25	5.25
1961	4.25	5.25
1961D	4.25	5.25
1962	4.25	5.25
1962D	4.25	5.25
1963	4.25	5.25
1963D	4.25	5.25

1962 Franklin Half Dollar

KENNEDY HALF DOLLARS

Only three days had elapsed between the assassination of President John F. Kennedy on Nov. 22, 1963, and the first notice from the U.S. Mint director to the chief engraver to prepare for the issue of a coin bearing Kennedy's portrait. To save time, Chief Engraver Gilroy Roberts based the obverse portrait on the Kennedy inaugural medal. The reverse is Frank Gasparro's rendition of the presidential seal. Remarkably, working dies were ready by Jan. 2, 1964.

Kennedy half dollars have been struck in three different compositions. The 1964 issue was struck in the traditional 90-percent silver alloy. The following year, when dimes and quarters were changed to cupronickel clad copper, the half dollar switched to a silver-clad version containing 80-percent silver in its outer layers and 21-percent silver in its middle layer. The remaining alloy was copper. Finally, silver in the half dollar was abandoned entirely in 1971, and only collector issues have been struck in that metal since.

Circulation issues are now struck in the same clad composition as dimes and quarters. Coins dated 1970D, 1987P and 1987D were not issued for circulation but are widely available from broken-up mint sets.

A special reverse was used in 1975 and 1976 (dated "1776-1976") to commemorate the U.S. Bicentennial. Designed by Seth G. Huntington, it depicts Independence Hall in Philadelphia.

Known Counterfeits: It is possible that none exist.

90-Percent-Silver Composition	MS-60
1964	6.00
1964D	6.25

40-Percent Silver Composition	MS-60
1965	3.00
1966	3.00
1967	3.00
1968D	3.00
1968S, proof	3.50
1969D	3.00
1969S, proof	3.75
1970D	13.00
1970S, proof	10.00

Clad Composition	MS-60
1971	1.00
1971D	1.00
1971S, proof	2.50
1972	1.00
1972D	1.00
1972S, proof	2.50
1973	1.00
1973D	1.50
1973S, proof	2.00

1964 Kennedy Half Dollar

Clad Composition	MS-60
1974	1.00
1974D	1.00
1974S, proof	1.75

Bicentennial Reverse	MS-60
1976, Bicentennial	1.00
1976D, Bicentennial	1.00
1976S, Bicentennial, proof	1.50
1976S, Bicentennial, 40-percent silver	4.00
1976S, Bicentennial, proof, 40-percent silver	3.00

Clad Composition (Non Bicentennial) Continued	MS-60
1977	1.25
1977D	1.35
1977S, proof	1.50
1978	1.75
1978D	2.25
1978S, proof	2.50
1979	1.25
1979D	1.25
1979, proof, type I	1.50
1979, proof, type II	12.50
1980P	1.00
1980D	1.00

1976D Kennedy Half Dollar with Bicentennial Reverse

Clad Composition (Non Bicentennial) Continued	MS-60
1980S, proof	1.75
1981P	1.25
1981D	1.25
1981S, proof	1.75
1982P	3.50
1982D	3.00
1982S, proof	2.25
1983P	4.50
1983D	4.75
1983S, proof	2.50
1984P	2.50
1984D	2.75
1984S, proof	3.50
1985P	3.00
1985D	2.50
1985S, proof	2.50
1986P	4.50
1986D	4.00
1986S, proof	3.50
1987P	3.00
1987D	2.50
1987S, proof	2.75
1988P	3.00

Clad Composition (Non Bicentennial) Continued	MS-60
1988D	2.00
1988S, proof	2.50
1989P	2.00
1989D	1.50
1989S, proof	4.00
1990P	2.00
1990D	3.00
1990S, proof	3.50
1991P	2.00
1991D	3.00
1991S, proof	9.00
1992P	1.25
1992D	2.25
1992S, proof	3.00
1992S, proof, silver	6.00
1993P	2.00
1993D	1.25
1993S, proof	8.50
1993S, proof, silver	20.00
1994P	1.00
1994D	1.50
1994S, proof	5.50
1994S, proof, silver	25.00

Clad Composition (Non Bicentennial) Continued	MS-60
1995P	1.00
1995D	1.00
1995S, proof	20.00
1995S, proof, silver	55.00
1996P	1.00
1996D	1.00
1996S, proof	8.00
1996S, proof, silver	25.00
1997P	1.00
1997D	1.00
1997S, proof	18.00
1997S, proof, silver	45.00
1998P	1.00
1998D	1.00
1998S, proof	10.00
1998S, matte proof, silver	240.00
1998S, proof, silver	14.00
1999P	1.75
1999D	1.75
1999S, proof	12.00
1999S, proof, silver	25.00
2000P	1.00
2000D	1.00

Clad Composition (Non Bicentennial) Continued	MS-60
2000S, proof	2.50
2000S, proof, silver	5.00
2001P	1.00
2001D	1.00
2001S, proof	5.50
2001S, proof, silver	12.00
2002P	1.50
2002D	1.75
2002S, proof	3.00
2002S, proof, silver	8.00
2003P	1.75
2003D	1.75
2003S, proof	2.00
2003S, proof, silver	5.00
2004P	1.85
2004D	1.85
2004S, proof	7.00
2004S, proof, silver	8.00
2005P	1.25
2005D	1.25
2005S, proof	2.00
2005S, proof, silver	5.00
2006P	1.50

2004S Proof Kennedy Half Dollar

Clad Composition (Non Bicentennial) Continued	MS-60
2006D	1.50
2006S, proof	3.50
2006S, proof, silver	6.00
2007P	1.75
2007D	1.75
2007S, proof	5.00
2007S, proof, silver	6.00
2008P	1.75
2008D	1.75
2008S, proof	5.00
2008S, proof, silver	6.00

SEATED LIBERTY DOLLARS

Production of silver dollars for circulation resumed in 1840 after a hiatus of 37 years. Seated Liberty silver dollars struck from 1853 to about 1867, however, were primarily intended as bullion pieces for export. Each contained more than a dollar's worth of silver. A ribbon with the motto "In God We Trust" was added over the eagle in 1866. These dollars are often found cleaned. Watch for retoned specimens as well.

Known Counterfeits: Counterfeits of this type are not common.

No Motto Above Eagle	F	XF
1840	330.00	500.00
1841	315.00	465.00
1842	315.00	465.00
1843	315.00	465.00
1844	360.00	785.00
1845	360.00	540.00
1846	345.00	650.00
1846O	370.00	650.00
1847	315.00	465.00
1848	475.00	1,200.00

1845 Seated Liberty Dollar with No Motto Above Eagle

No Motto Above Eagle	F	XF
1849	330.00	500.00
1850	645.00	1,750.00
1850O	500.00	1,550.00
1851	5,750.00	18,000.00
1851, proof, restrike	—	21,000.00
1852	5,200.00	15,000.00
1852, proof, restrike	—	20,000.00
1853	550.00	875.00
1854	2,000.00	4,500.00
1855	1,450.00	3,750.00
1856	650.00	1,650.00
1857	675.00	1,500.00
1858, proof, restrike	4,000.00	7,250.00
1859	390.00	635.00
1859O	315.00	465.00
1859S	510.00	1,550.00
1860	330.00	500.00
1860O	315.00	465.00
1861	900.00	1,500.00
1862	850.00	1,350.00
1863	575.00	975.00
1864	500.00	900.00

No Motto Above Eagle	F	XF
1865	420.00	900.00
1866, no motto, two known	—	—

Motto Above Eagle	F	XF
1866	390.00	555.00
1867	385.00	550.00
1868	370.00	535.00
1869	395.00	560.00
1870	340.00	500.00
1870CC	765.00	2,250.00
1870S, 12-15 known	—	April 1997 auction, $250,000.00
1871	330.00	500.00
1871CC	4,400.00	14,000.00
1872	330.00	500.00
1872CC	2,650.00	7,250.00
1872S	550.00	2,000.00
1873	340.00	510.00
1873CC	11,500.00	32,500.00
1873S, none known	—	—

1871 Seated Liberty Dollar with Motto Above Eagle

TRADE DOLLARS

Trade dollars were struck for export as bullion, usually to the Far East. They were largely intended to compete against the Mexican peso, which had slightly more silver than a standard dollar. The U.S. coins were distinguished by a Liberty and eagle facing in the opposite direction from the standard dollars.

From the beginning, the legal-tender status of Trade dollars was limited in the United States, but in 1876, when the price of silver dropped, they ceased to be legal tender altogether until their status was restored in 1965. Eight million were redeemed by the government in 1887. Only proof examples were struck from 1879 to 1885.

It was common for Asian merchants to impress a character into Trade dollars and other silver coins to confirm that they accepted them as good quality. These "chop marks" are commonly found on Trade dollars, sometimes in quantity. They reduce a coin's value because they are considered a form of mutilation, but the marks have recently been the subject of serious research. Chop-marked dollars may not be as valuable as unmarked examples, but they are still collectible.

Known Counterfeits: Counterfeits are not abundant and are more likely to be contemporary. Watch for cleaned coins.

1876 Trade Dollar

	F	XF
1873	145.00	250.00
1873CC	330.00	700.00
1873S	155.00	265.00
1874	150.00	250.00
1874CC	310.00	600.00
1874S	140.00	175.00
1875	375.00	590.00
1875CC	285.00	510.00
1875S	130.00	165.00
1875S, S over CC	375.00	925.00
1876	140.00	175.00
1876CC	300.00	525.00
1876S	130.00	165.00
1877	140.00	175.00
1877CC	320.00	700.00
1877S	130.00	165.00
1878, proof	—	1,300.00
1878CC	710.00	2,400.00
1878S	130.00	165.00
1879, proof	—	1,250.00
1880, proof	—	1,250.00
1881, proof	—	1,300.00
1882, proof	—	1,275.00

	F	XF
1883, proof	—	1,300.00
1884, proof	—	April 1997 auction, $396,000
1885, proof	—	April 1997 auction, $907,500

MORGAN DOLLARS

The Morgan dollar was introduced in response to pressure from silver-mining interests. For decades, silver dollars were scarce in circulation. With the boom in silver mining, the price of the metal dropped as supplies increased. Something needed to be done to remove the excess silver from the market.

The new design coincided with the reintroduction of circulating silver dollars after a five-year absence. Because they were inconvenient, however, perhaps hundreds of thousands of these dollars sat for decades in bags held as private, bank, and government reserves. The U.S. Treasury was stuck with such an excess that thousands remained on hand for almost a century, prompting the famous General Services Administration auction of silver dollars in the 1970s. Those coins in distinctive GSA cases often command a slight premium.

Artistically, many consider the Morgan dollar, named after its designer, George T. Morgan, an aesthetically pleasing but unoriginal design. Morgan's competence (and perhaps his interesting use of Gothic script) may be attributed to his training at the British Royal Mint in London.

A long gap exists between the 1904 issue and the last Morgan issue in 1921. During this time, the master dies were lost and new ones had to be prepared. As a result, there are subtle differences in relief on the 1921 issues. They are less pleasing, and dealers often pay less for this date than they do for other Morgan dollars in bulk. Strike quality can also vary from mint to mint. San Francisco Mint examples are usually fully struck, Philadelphia strikes are of medium quality, and New Orleans dollars are usually the most weakly struck. These differences are usually most obvious on the eagle's breast.

Morgans have been among the most popular investment coins. This is partially because of their availability in great quantities in uncirculated condition, the typical grade favored by investment promoters and investors. It is ironic that their sheer commonness has contributed to their desirability.

Known Counterfeits: Genuine coins have been altered to pass for 1879CC, 1889CC, 1892S, 1893S, 1894, 1895, 1895S, 1896S, 1901, 1903S, and 1904S issues. Cast counterfeits are known of 1878, 1878S, 1879S, 1880O, 1881, 1883, 1883S, 1885, 1888O, 1889, 1889O, 1892O, 1899O, 1901, 1902, 1903, 1904S,

1921D, and 1921S. Struck counterfeits of certain rare dates are also possible. Cleaned coins are common and are heavily discounted, as are scuffed and heavily edge-knocked pieces. Be careful to avoid coins with false toning.

	VF	MS-60
1878, eight tail feathers	38.00	130.00
1878, 7 over 8 tail feathers	30.00	145.00
1878, seven feathers	23.00	75.00
1878, seven tail feathers, reverse of 1879	25.00	80.00
1878CC	110.00	225.00
1878S	25.00	60.00
1879	20.00	30.00
1879CC	285.00	4,150.00
1879O	20.00	75.00
1879S	25.00	125.00
1880	20.00	30.00
1880CC	250.00	575.00
1880O	20.00	60.00
1880S	20.00	30.00
1881	20.00	28.00
1881CC	410.00	555.00
1881O	20.00	40.00
1881S	20.00	30.00

1881CC Morgan Dollar

	VF	MS-60
1882	20.00	32.00
1882CC	110.00	220.00
1882O	20.00	40.00
1882O, O over S	50.00	255.00
1882S	20.00	30.00
1883	20.00	28.00
1883CC	110.00	215.00
1883O	20.00	25.00
1883S	20.00	635.00
1884	20.00	28.00
1884CC	160.00	215.00
1884O	20.00	26.00
1884S	20.00	5,750.00
1885	20.00	25.00
1885CC	600.00	650.00
1885O	20.00	25.00
1885S	40.00	240.00
1886	20.00	25.00
1886O	18.00	565.00
1886S	85.00	285.00
1887, 7 over 6	35.00	425.00
1887	20.00	50.00
1887O, 7 over 6	40.00	450.00

18870 Morgan Dollar

	VF	MS-60
1887O	20.00	50.00
1887S	20.00	110.00
1888	20.00	28.00
1888O	20.00	28.00
1888S	210.00	300.00
1889	20.00	27.00
1889CC	1,500.00	21,500.00
1889O	20.00	135.00
1889S	65.00	210.00
1890	20.00	28.00
1890CC	110.00	450.00
1890O	20.00	60.00
1890S	20.00	55.00
1891	20.00	50.00
1891CC	100.00	360.00
1891O	20.00	135.00
1891S	20.00	55.00
1892	23.00	155.00
1892CC	290.00	1,650.00
1892O	23.00	160.00
1892S	135.00	34,500.00
1893	260.00	750.00
1893CC	725.00	3,700.00

1892S Morgan Dollar

	VF	MS-60
1893O	380.00	2,250.00
1893S	7,250.00	90,000.00
1894	1,850.00	4,950.00
1894O	70.00	580.00
1894S	110.00	695.00
1895, proof	29,000.00	—
1895O	595.00	17,000.00
1895S	775.00	4,150.00
1896	20.00	28.00
1896O	20.00	1,450.00
1896S	60.00	1,775.00
1897	20.00	28.00
1897O	20.00	735.00
1897S	20.00	60.00
1898	20.00	28.00
1898O	23.00	30.00
1898S	35.00	260.00
1899	215.00	295.00
1899O	20.00	28.00
1899S	38.00	320.00
1900	20.00	28.00
1900O	20.00	28.00
1900O, O over CC	63.00	350.00

	VF	MS-60
1900S	25.00	325.00
1901	58.00	2,200.00
1901O	20.00	28.00
1901S	30.00	470.00
1902	20.00	45.00
1902O	20.00	27.00
1902S	160.00	425.00
1903	50.00	75.00
1903O	375.00	425.00
1903S	215.00	4,400.00
1904	25.00	80.00
1904O	25.00	35.00
1904S	85.00	1,075.00
1921	15.00	18.00
1921D	15.00	45.00
1921S	15.00	45.00

1901 Morgan Dollar

PEACE DOLLARS

Like the Morgan dollar before it, the Peace dollar was the result of a congressional mandate for a new large coinage of silver dollars. When the famous numismatist Farran Zerbe learned that this new issue of dollars was to bear the old Morgan design, he pushed for a new, artistically more progressive replacement. The result was a new radiant Liberty head by sculptor Anthony de Francisci that also commemorated the end of World War I. The word "Peace" can be seen on the rocky perch on which the eagle stands. The first Peace dollars, dated 1921, were struck in a much higher relief than subsequent issues were.

The traditional silver dollar was last struck for circulation in 1935. In 1965, several hundred thousand 1964-dated Peace dollars were struck at the Denver Mint but were later melted. None has been officially verified, but there have long been rumors, generally accepted by the numismatic community, that several escaped the Mint's melting pot.

Like the Morgan dollar, this coin is available in mint state in abundant quantities. The broad, smooth surfaces, however, made many mint-state pieces susceptible to unsightly bruises and bag marks.

Known Counterfeits: 1928 examples altered from authentic 1923 or 1928S examples, as well as other counterfeits of this date, are known.

1921 Peace Dollar

	VF	MS-60
1921	140.00	270.00
1922	15.00	17.00
1922D	14.00	27.00
1922S	14.00	27.00
1923	14.00	17.00
1923D	17.00	50.00
1923S	14.00	28.00
1924	14.00	17.00
1924S	35.00	200.00
1925	14.00	23.00
1925S	30.00	75.00
1926	16.00	45.00
1926D	15.00	65.00
1926S	15.00	45.00
1927	35.00	70.00
1927D	30.00	150.00
1927S	32.00	150.00
1928	455.00	525.00
1928S	40.00	155.00
1934	21.00	120.00
1934D	22.00	135.00
1934S	85.00	1,800.00
1935	22.00	60.00

	VF	MS-60
1935S	22.00	235.00
1964D, none known	—	—

EISENHOWER DOLLARS

The "Ike" dollar commemorates the first manned moon landing in 1969, as well as the World War II general and later president. The coin's reverse was an adaptation of the Apollo XI insignia, depicting an eagle clutching an olive branch and landing on the moon. The obverse shows a left-facing portrait of Dwight D. Eisenhower.

Circulation strikes were of the same cupronickel clad composition as the dime and quarter. Special collector issues were also struck in a silver clad version similar to the alloy used for the half dollars of 1965-1970. These special silver coins, bearing the "S" mintmark, were released in blue envelopes for the uncirculated issues and brown boxes for the proofs. Most dealers and collectors require that they be in the original packaging.

A special reverse commemorated the U.S. Bicentennial. It featured the Liberty Bell superimposed on the moon, as arranged by design contest winner Dennis R. Williams. Bicentennial dollars were struck in 1975 and 1976, and are dated "1776-1976." Those struck in 1975 have heavy block lettering; those struck in 1976 used slightly finer letters.

Known Counterfeits: Poor quality counterfeits have recently come out of Communist China. Specifically, 1976D counterfeits are known.

	MS-63	PF-65
1971	10.00	—
1971D	8.00	—
1971S, 40-percent silver	7.50	11.00
1972	6.50	—
1972D	5.50	—
1972S, 40-percent silver	7.50	14.00
1973	14.00	—
1973D	15.00	—
1973S, proof	—	12.00
1973S, 40-percent silver	8.50	35.00
1974	5.50	—
1974D	7.00	—
1974S, proof	—	11.00
1974S, 40-percent silver	7.50	14.00
Bicentennial Reverse	**MS-63**	**PF-65**
1976, type I	9.00	—
1976, type II	5.00	—
1976D, type I	6.00	—

1974D Eisenhower Dollar

1976D Eisenhower Dollar with Bicentennial Reverse

Type I, Squared "T"   *Type II, Slant-top "T"*

Bicentennial Reverse	MS-63	PF-65
1976D, type II	5.00	—
1976S, type I	—	13.00
1976S, type II	—	9.00
1976S, 40-percent silver, type I	12.50	20.00

	MS-63	PF-65
1977	7.00	—
1977D	7.00	—
1977S	—	10.00
1978	5.00	—
1978D	5.00	—
1978S	—	12.00

ANTHONY DOLLARS

The smaller Anthony dollar was intended to save the government money by replacing paper dollars with the longer-lasting coin. The vending-machine industry also pushed for its release. The large "Ike" dollars were inconvenient for vending machines, but a coin of its value was necessary to facilitate the sale of more expensive items in machines.

Its obverse depicts U.S. Mint Chief Engraver Frank Gasparro's portrait of Susan B. Anthony, who was instrumental in gaining women the right to vote. The reverse design is the same Apollo XI motif used on the Eisenhower dollar.

One of the least popular coins in U.S. history, it was often confused with the quarter because of their size similarity. It was also struck in the same clad composition as the quarter. After only two years of circulation production, Anthony dollars were struck for mint sets only in 1981. Circulation production resumed for one year in 1999 as new demand from the vending-machine industry and mass-transit authorities drew down Mint inventories of the coin.

Known Counterfeits: Not common.

	MS-63	PF-65
1979P, narrow rim, far date	2.50	—
1979P, wide rim, near date	70.00	—
1979D	3.00	—

1979D Anthony Dollar

	MS-63	PF-65
1979S	3.00	—
1979S, type I	—	8.00
1979S, type II	—	110.00
1980D	3.00	—
1980S	3.50	8.00
1981D	7.50	—
1981S	7.50	—
1981S, filled S	—	8.00
1981S, clear S	—	230.00
1999P	4.00	25.00
1999D	4.00	—

SACAGAWEA DOLLARS

The Sacagawea dollar coin tried to correct the problems associated with the Anthony dollar. To distinguish it from the quarter, the Sacagawea dollar has a plain edge instead of reeded, a wider border than other circulating coins have, and a golden color.

The coin depicts Sacagawea, the Shoshone Indian guide and translator who accompanied Lewis and Clark on their exploration of the American West in the early 1800s. She carries her infant son on her back. Glenna Goodacre designed the obverse. The reverse, designed by Thomas D. Rogers Jr., depicts a graceful eagle in flight.

Although the same size as the Anthony dollar, the Sacagawea dollar has a unique composition of 77-percent copper, 12-percent zinc, seven-percent manganese, and four-percent nickel bonded to a pure copper core. This coin is prone to spotting. Mint-state examples lacking spots are more desirable.

Known Counterfeits: Examples primarily made for circulation in Ecuador are known.

	MS-63	PF-65
2000P	2.00	—
2000D	2.00	—
2000S	—	10.00
2001P	2.00	—
2001D	2.00	—
2001S	—	100.00
2002P	2.00	—

2002P Sacagawea Dollar

	MS-63	PF-65
2002D	2.00	—
2002S	—	29.00
2003P	3.00	—
2003D	3.00	—
2003S	—	20.00
2004P	2.50	—
2004D	2.50	—
2004S	—	22.50
2005P	2.50	—
2005D	2.50	—
2005S	—	22.50
2006P	2.50	—
2006D	5.00	—
2006S	—	22.50
2007P	2.50	—
2007D	2.50	—
2007S	—	22.50
2008P	2.50	—
2008D	2.50	—
2008S	—	22.50

PRESIDENTIAL DOLLARS

Following on the heels of the popular 50 State Quarters, Congress authorized the Presidential Dollar Coin Series, which began in 2007. Four presidents will be honored each year in the order in which they served. The final two, Richard M. Nixon and Gerald R. Ford, are scheduled to conclude the series in 2016.

The coins' reverse depicts the Statue of Liberty. Composition is the same as the Sacagawea dollar.

A distinctive feature of the Presidential coins is incuse edge lettering. Lettered edges have been used occasionally on U.S. coins in the past, but most have used raised lettering, not incuse. Even more unusual is the location of the date and mintmark on the edge along with the motto "In God We Trust." The edges, however, have been susceptible to errors, most often doubling. These errors have attracted much public attention. Prices for them soared just a few weeks after their discovery. Not all dealers, however, are willing to buy them. Many are concerned that these high prices are a passing fad.

Presidential dollars are collected almost exclusively in mint-state condition.

Known Counterfeits: So far, counterfeits have not plagued this series, despite the interest in the unusual edges.

George Washington	MS-63
2007P	2.00
2007D	2.00
2007S	—
ND (2007), plain edge error	75.00

John Adams	MS-63
2007P	2.00
2007P, double-edge lettering	250.00
2007D	2.00
2007S	—

Thomas Jefferson	MS-63
2007P	2.00
2007D	2.00
2007S	—

James Madison	MS-63
2007P	2.00
2007D	2.00
2007S	—

George Washington

John Adams

Presidential
Dollar Reverse

James Madison

Thomas Jefferson

James Monroe

John Quincy Adams

Andrew Jackson

Martin Van Buren

James Monroe	MS-63
2008P	2.00
2008D	2.00
2008S	—
ND (2007), plain edge error	75.00

John Quincy Adams	MS-63
2008P	2.00
2008P, double-edge lettering	250.00
2008D	2.00
2008S	—

Andrew Jackson	MS-63
2008P	2.00
2008D	2.00
2008S	—

Martin Van Buren	MS-63
2008P	2.00
2008D	2.00
2008S	—

QUARTER EAGLES (GOLD $2.50)

The first quarter eagles were struck in 1796, one year after the first U.S. gold coins—half eagles and eagles—were struck. The quarter eagle was the first U.S. coin to depict a heraldic eagle with a shield on its chest, which later was featured on all denominations other than copper.

Its first obverse featured a bust of Liberty wearing a tall conical cap, traditionally but inaccurately referred to by numismatists as a turban. This first bust, by designer Robert Scot, was replaced by one designed by John Reich, which had a smaller cap. A reverse eagle similar to the one on the first quarter eagle, but more realistic, was paired with the new obverse. No quarter eagles were struck from 1809 until 1821, when production resumed with the same specifications except for a slightly smaller diameter.

Through most of its history until the 1830s, quarter eagles were widely melted because they were undervalued relative to their gold content, particularly by European standards. This was remedied in 1834 by reducing their gold content. This was indicated to the public by the removal of the motto over the eagle on the reverse and by a new, capless Liberty head, the "Classic Head" by designer William Kneass.

The final coronet-type Liberty head design was a rendition by Christian Gobrecht, which continued from 1840 to 1907.

Pieces dated 1848 and countermarked "CAL." were struck with gold shipped east by the military governor of California.

In 1908, as part of the same coin design beautification program that later introduced the Walking Liberty half dollar and Saint-Gaudens double eagle, sculptor Bela Lyon Pratt was asked to prepare new designs for the quarter eagle and half eagle in secret under the authority of President Theodore Roosevelt. His work showed the bust of an Indian chief on the obverse and an eagle with closed wings on the reverse. It was both controversial and innovative because its design was in relief but recessed below the coin's surface. Some criticized it for aesthetic reasons and others for fear that dirt trapped in the recesses would spread germs, but the technique shielded the design from wear.

Known Counterfeits: Examples of the 1848 "CAL.," 1875, and 1911D made by altering genuine coins of other dates or mints exist. Struck counterfeits of virtually every date in this series exist. All examples dated 1905S are counterfeit. Be cautious of false "C" mintmarks made by cutting down an authentic "O" mintmark. Beware of traces of solder on earlier coins used as jewelry. Look for interruption in the pattern of edge reeding. Be cautious of cleaned coins, which are harder to detect in gold because it usually does not tone naturally.

Classic Head	VF	XF
1834, no motto above eagle	475.00	675.00
1835	475.00	675.00
1836	475.00	675.00
1837	500.00	800.00
1838	500.00	625.00
1838C	1,700.00	3,000.00
1839	500.00	900.00
1839C	1,500.00	2,650.00
1839D	1,750.00	3,450.00
1839O	700.00	1,100.00

Coronet Type	F	XF
1840	160.00	900.00
1840C	975.00	1,600.00
1840D	2,000.00	8,700.00
1840O	250.00	825.00
1841	—	85,000.00
1841C	750.00	2,000.00
1841D	950.00	4,750.00
1842	500.00	2,600.00
1842C	700.00	3,500.00
1842D	900.00	4,000.00
1842O	240.00	1,200.00
1843	160.00	450.00

1834 Gold $2.50 with Classic Head (No Motto)

18420 Gold $2.50 with Coronet (No Motto)

Coronet Type	F	XF
1843C, crosslet 4, small date	1,500.00	5,500.00
1843C, plain 4, large date	800.00	2,200.00
1843D	920.00	2,350.00
1843O, crosslet 4, small date	165.00	250.00
1843O, plain 4, large date	210.00	465.00
1844	225.00	850.00
1844C	700.00	2,600.00
1844D	785.00	2,200.00
1845	190.00	350.00
1845D	950.00	2,600.00
1845O	550.00	2,300.00
1846	200.00	500.00
1846C	725.00	3,500.00
1846D	800.00	2,000.00
1846O	170.00	400.00
1847	140.00	360.00
1847C	900.00	2,300.00
1847D	800.00	2,250.00
1847O	160.00	400.00
1848	315.00	850.00
1848, "CAL"	8,000.00	26,000.00
1848C	800.00	2,100.00
1848D	1,000.00	2,500.00

Coronet Type	F	XF
1849	180.00	475.00
1849C	800.00	2,150.00
1849D	950.00	2,500.00
1850	160.00	275.00
1850C	800.00	2,100.00
1850D	950.00	2,500.00
1850O	170.00	450.00
1851	145.00	200.00
1851C	900.00	2,300.00
1851D	950.00	2,600.00
1851O	160.00	220.00
1852	150.00	200.00
1852C	675.00	2,100.00
1852D	840.00	2,800.00
1852O	160.00	300.00
1853	150.00	200.00
1853D	950.00	3,400.00
1854	150.00	215.00
1854C	800.00	2,400.00
1854D	1,750.00	6,950.00
1854O	150.00	240.00
1854S	32,500.00	115,000.00
1855	145.00	225.00

Coronet Type	F	XF
1855C	800.00	3,300.00
1855D	1,750.00	7,500.00
1856	145.00	210.00
1856C	650.00	2,200.00
1856D	3,500.00	12,500.00
1856O	180.00	750.00
1856S	160.00	375.00
1857	150.00	205.00
1857D	875.00	2,900.00
1857O	155.00	350.00
1857S	160.00	340.00
1858	150.00	250.00
1858C	825.00	2,100.00
1859	150.00	265.00
1859D	1,000.00	3,300.00
1859S	200.00	1,000.00
1860	150.00	265.00
1860C	815.00	2,200.00
1860S	170.00	675.00
1861	150.00	210.00
1861S	200.00	1,000.00
1862, 2 over 1	450.00	2,000.00
1862	160.00	300.00

1859 Gold $2.50 with Coronet (No Motto)

Coronet Type	F	XF
1862S	500.00	2,100.00
1863, proof	—	35,000.00
1863S	250.00	1,500.00
1864	2,500.00	8,800.00
1865	2,400.00	8,000.00
1865S	160.00	650.00
1866	650.00	3,500.00
1866S	180.00	650.00
1867	190.00	900.00
1867S	170.00	625.00
1868	170.00	400.00
1868S	150.00	300.00
1869	170.00	450.00
1869S	160.00	440.00
1870	165.00	425.00
1870S	155.00	400.00
1871	160.00	325.00
1871S	150.00	280.00
1872	200.00	750.00
1872S	155.00	415.00
1873, closed 3	155.00	210.00
1873, open 3	155.00	195.00
1873S	160.00	425.00

Coronet Type	F	XF
1874	170.00	380.00
1875	1,750.00	5,000.00
1875S	150.00	300.00
1876	170.00	675.00
1876S	170.00	525.00
1877	275.00	800.00
1877S	150.00	200.00
1878	150.00	200.00
1878S	150.00	200.00
1879	150.00	195.00
1879S	155.00	300.00
1880	170.00	335.00
1881	900.00	3,400.00
1882	160.00	290.00
1883	175.00	440.00
1884	175.00	420.00
1885	400.00	1,800.00
1886	170.00	270.00
1887	175.00	245.00
1888	160.00	240.00
1889	155.00	230.00
1890	170.00	240.00
1891	165.00	215.00

1875 Gold $2.50 with Coronet (No Motto)

Coronet Type	F	XF
1892	170.00	250.00
1893	165.00	200.00
1894	170.00	225.00
1895	150.00	225.00
1896	150.00	225.00
1897	150.00	210.00
1898	150.00	210.00
1899	150.00	210.00
1900	150.00	250.00
1901	150.00	200.00
1902	150.00	200.00
1903	150.00	200.00
1904	150.00	200.00
1905	150.00	200.00
1906	150.00	200.00
1907	150.00	195.00

Indian	VF	AU
1908	165.00	230.00
1909	175.00	230.00
1910	175.00	230.00
1911	175.00	230.00
1911D	2,500.00	5,000.00
1912	175.00	230.00

1911D Gold $2.50 with Indian Head

Indian	VF	AU
1913	175.00	230.00
1914	175.00	260.00
1914D	175.00	230.00
1915	175.00	230.00
1925D	175.00	230.00
1926	175.00	230.00
1927	175.00	230.00
1928	175.00	230.00
1929	180.00	250.00

HALF EAGLES (GOLD $5)

The first U.S. gold coins were 1795 half eagles. The obverse featured a bust of Liberty wearing a tall conical cap traditionally but inaccurately referred to by numismatists as a turban. Originally this was paired with a reverse design featuring a skinny eagle similar to the one on the first silver dollars. Instead of standing within a wreath, however, it holds a wreath above its head on the half eagle. As with other denominations, the skinny eagle was replaced by a plumper, heraldic eagle bearing a shield on its chest, which later was featured on all denominations other than copper.

The original bust by designer Robert Scot was replaced in 1807 by one designed by John Reich, which wore a smaller cap. A reverse eagle that is similar to the one on the first half eagle, but more realistic, was paired with the new obverse. Although the design and net gold content did not change for almost 30 years, the coin's diameter was at first increased and then later reduced.

Through most of its history until the 1830s, the quarter eagle was widely melted because it was undervalued relative to its gold content, particularly by European standards. This was remedied in 1834 by reducing the coin's gold content. This was indicated to the public by the removal of the motto over the eagle on the reverse and by a new capless Liberty head, the "Classic Head" by William Kneass. The final coronet-type Liberty-head design was a rendition by Christian Gobrecht, which continued from 1839 to 1908. The motto "In God We Trust" was added to the reverse above the eagle in 1866.

In 1908, as part of the same coin design beautification program that later introduced the Walking Liberty half dollar and Saint-Gaudens double eagle, sculptor Bela Lyon Pratt was asked to prepare new designs for the quarter eagle and half eagle in secret under the authority of President Theodore Roosevelt. His work showed the bust of an Indian chief on the obverse and an eagle with closed wings on the reverse. It was both controversial and innovative because the design was in relief but recessed below the coin's surface. Some criticized it for aesthetic reasons and others for fear that dirt trapped in the recesses would spread germs, but the technique shielded the design from wear.

Known Counterfeits: 1811, 1815 (altered), 1841O (probable), 1852C, 1854S (altered), 1858, 1870CC (altered), 1875, 1877 (altered), 1885, 1885S, 1887 Proof (altered), 1892, 1892O (altered), 1906S, 1907D, 1908 (Liberty), 1908D, 1909 Matte Proof, 1909D, 1909O, 1910D, 1914D, 1914S, and 1915D (all counterfeit), among others. Be cautious of false "C" mintmarks altered by cutting down an authentic "O" mintmark. Beware of traces of solder on earlier coins used as jewelry. Look for interruption in the pattern of edge reeding. Be cautious of cleaned coins, which are harder to detect on gold because it usually does not tone naturally.

Classic Head	VF	XF
1834, no motto above eagle, plain 4	390.00	550.00
1834, no motto above eagle, crosslet 4	1,650.00	2,900.00
1835	390.00	560.00
1836	390.00	550.00
1837	390.00	585.00
1838	390.00	550.00
1838C	2,200.00	4,000.00
1838D	2,000.00	3,850.00

Coronet	VF	XF
1839	275.00	480.00
1839C	2,300.00	2,900.00
1839D	2,200.00	3,200.00
1840	230.00	360.00
1840C	2,200.00	3,000.00
1840D	2,200.00	3,000.00
1840O	365.00	875.00
1841	400.00	875.00
1841C	1,850.00	2,400.00
1841D	1,800.00	2,350.00
1841O, two known	—	—
1842, small letters	345.00	1,100.00
1842, large letters	750.00	2,000.00

1834 Gold $5 with
Classic Head and Crosslet 4 (No Motto)

Coronet	VF	XF
1842C, small date	10,000.00	23,000.00
1842C, large date	1,800.00	2,200.00
1842D, small letters	2,000.00	2,300.00
1842D, large letters	2,350.00	6,500.00
1842O	1,000.00	3,400.00
1843	230.00	330.00
1843C	1,850.00	2,500.00
1843D	1,950.00	2,600.00
1843O, small letters	660.00	1,700.00
1843O, large letters	265.00	1,175.00
1844	230.00	330.00
1844C	1,900.00	3,000.00
1844D	1,950.00	2,400.00
1844O	250.00	375.00
1845	235.00	260.00
1845D	1,900.00	2,400.00
1845O	415.00	800.00
1846, small date	220.00	240.00
1846	230.00	330.00
1846C	1,900.00	3,000.00
1846D	1,800.00	2,400.00
1846O	375.00	1,000.00

1841 Gold $5 with Coronet (No Motto)

Coronet	VF	XF
1847	230.00	250.00
1847C	1,800.00	2,400.00
1847D	2,000.00	4,000.00
1847O	2,200.00	6,750.00
1848	230.00	275.00
1848C	1,900.00	2,250.00
1848D	2,000.00	2,350.00
1849	230.00	280.00
1849C	1,900.00	2,400.00
1849D	2,000.00	2,600.00
1850	300.00	625.00
1850C	1,850.00	2,300.00
1850D	1,950.00	2,500.00
1851	230.00	250.00
1851C	1,900.00	2,350.00
1851D	1,950.00	2,400.00
1851O	590.00	1,500.00
1852	230.00	260.00
1852C	1,900.00	2,450.00
1852D	2,000.00	2,450.00
1853	230.00	250.00
1853C	1,950.00	2,350.00

Coronet	VF	XF
1853D	2,000.00	2,500.00
1854	230.00	260.00
1854C	1,900.00	2,300.00
1854D	1,875.00	2,200.00
1854O	300.00	525.00
1854S	—	October 1982 auction, $170,000
1855	230.00	250.00
1855C	1,900.00	2,300.00
1855D	1,950.00	2,400.00
1855O	675.00	2,100.00
1855S	390.00	1,000.00
1856	230.00	240.00
1856C	1,875.00	2,400.00
1856D	1,950.00	2,600.00
1856O	650.00	1,600.00
1856S	300.00	700.00
1857	230.00	260.00
1857C	1,900.00	2,500.00
1857D	2,000.00	2,650.00
1857O	640.00	1,400.00
1857S	300.00	700.00

1851 Gold $5 with Coronet (No Motto)

Coronet	VF	XF
1858	240.00	550.00
1858C	1,900.00	2,350.00
1858D	2,000.00	2,450.00
1858S	825.00	2,350.00
1859	325.00	625.00
1859C	1,900.00	2,450.00
1859D	2,150.00	2,600.00
1859S	1,800.00	4,150.00
1860	280.00	575.00
1860C	2,100.00	3,000.00
1860D	1,900.00	2,600.00
1860S	1,100.00	2,100.00
1861	230.00	245.00
1861C	2,400.00	3,900.00
1861D	4,700.00	7,000.00
1861S	1,100.00	4,500.00
1862	800.00	1,850.00
1862S	3,000.00	6,300.00
1863	1,200.00	3,750.00
1863S	1,450.00	4,100.00
1864	650.00	1,850.00
1864S	4,750.00	16,000.00

1858 Gold $5 with Coronet (No Motto)

Coronet	VF	XF
1865	1,450.00	4,100.00
1865S	1,400.00	2,400.00
1866S, no motto on reverse	1,750.00	4,000.00

Coronet, motto above eagle	VF	XF
1866	800.00	1,650.00
1866S	900.00	2,600.00
1867	500.00	1,500.00
1867S	1,400.00	2,900.00
1868	650.00	1,000.00
1868S	400.00	1,550.00
1869	925.00	2,400.00
1869S	500.00	1,750.00
1870	800.00	2,000.00
1870CC	5,250.00	15,000.00
1870S	950.00	2,600.00
1871	950.00	1,700.00
1871CC	1,250.00	3,000.00
1871S	500.00	950.00
1872	850.00	1,925.00
1872CC	1,250.00	5,000.00
1872S	460.00	800.00
1873, closed 3	215.00	225.00

Coronet, motto above eagle	VF	XF
1873, open 3	215.00	220.00
1873CC	2,600.00	12,500.00
1873S	525.00	1,400.00
1874	660.00	1,675.00
1874CC	850.00	1,750.00
1874S	640.00	2,100.00
1875	34,000.00	45,000.00
1875CC	1,400.00	4,500.00
1875S	715.00	2,250.00
1876	1,100.00	2,500.00
1876CC	1,450.00	5,000.00
1876S	2,000.00	3,600.00
1877	900.00	2,750.00
1877CC	1,000.00	3,300.00
1877S	400.00	650.00
1878	230.00	240.00
1878CC	3,100.00	7,200.00
1878S	230.00	235.00
1879	230.00	235.00
1879CC	575.00	1,500.00
1879S	235.00	240.00
1880	225.00	230.00
1880CC	425.00	815.00

Coronet, motto above eagle	VF	XF
1880S	225.00	230.00
1881, 1 over 0	330.00	600.00
1881	225.00	230.00
1881CC	550.00	1,500.00
1881S	225.00	230.00
1882	225.00	230.00
1882CC	415.00	625.00
1882S	225.00	230.00
1883	240.00	245.00
1883CC	460.00	1,100.00
1883S	240.00	245.00
1884	240.00	245.00
1884CC	550.00	975.00
1884S	240.00	245.00
1885	225.00	230.00
1885S	225.00	230.00
1886	225.00	230.00
1886S	225.00	230.00
1887, proof	—	14,500.00
1887S	225.00	230.00
1888	240.00	245.00
1888S	230.00	235.00
1889	350.00	440.00

1866 Gold $5 with Coronet and Motto

1884S Gold $5 with Coronet and Motto

Coronet, motto above eagle	VF	XF
1890	400.00	475.00
1890CC	330.00	460.00
1891	240.00	240.00
1891CC	325.00	415.00
1892	225.00	230.00
1892CC	340.00	400.00
1892O	515.00	1,000.00
1892S	225.00	230.00
1893	225.00	230.00
1893CC	360.00	465.00
1893O	240.00	340.00
1893S	225.00	230.00
1894	225.00	230.00
1894O	245.00	360.00
1894S	250.00	375.00
1895	225.00	230.00
1895S	230.00	275.00
1896	225.00	230.00
1896S	235.00	240.00
1897	225.00	230.00
1897S	225.00	230.00
1898	225.00	230.00
1898S	225.00	230.00

Coronet, motto above eagle	VF	XF
1899	225.00	230.00
1899S	225.00	230.00
1900	225.00	230.00
1900S	225.00	230.00
1901	225.00	230.00
1901S	225.00	230.00
1901S	225.00	230.00
1902	225.00	230.00
1902S	225.00	230.00
1903	225.00	230.00
1903S	225.00	230.00
1904	225.00	230.00
1904S	235.00	240.00
1905	225.00	230.00
1905S	225.00	230.00
1906	225.00	230.00
1906D	225.00	230.00
1906S	225.00	230.00
1907	225.00	230.00
1907D	225.00	230.00
1908	225.00	230.00

Indian	VF	XF
1908	280.00	290.00

1899 Gold $5 with Coronet and Motto

Indian	VF	XF
1908D	280.00	290.00
1908S	355.00	365.00
1909	280.00	290.00
1909D	280.00	290.00
1909O	2,150.00	3,350.00
1909S	310.00	330.00
1910	280.00	290.00
1910D	280.00	290.00
1910S	320.00	345.00
1911	280.00	290.00
1911D	575.00	700.00
1911S	290.00	325.00
1912	280.00	290.00
1912S	325.00	355.00
1913	280.00	290.00
1913S	320.00	350.00
1914	280.00	290.00
1914D	280.00	290.00
1914S	325.00	345.00
1915	280.00	290.00
1915S	335.00	365.00
1916S	300.00	325.00
1929	7,500.00	10,750.00

1908 Gold $5 with Indian Head

EAGLES (GOLD $10)

President George Washington received the first example of this coin struck in 1795. Its obverse features a bust of Liberty by designer Robert Scot. She wears a tall conical cap traditionally but inaccurately referred to by numismatists as a turban. Originally this was paired with a reverse design featuring a skinny eagle similar to the one on the first silver dollars. Instead of standing within a wreath, however, it holds a wreath above its head. As with other denominations, the skinny eagle was replaced by a plumper heraldic eagle bearing a shield on its chest, which later was featured on all denominations other than those struck in copper.

Early eagles were struck on a primitive screw press with hand-engraved dies, no two of which were identical. Many have adjustment marks, a scraping of metal from the blank before striking to prevent the coin from being overweight. Although not desirable, they are not considered damaged because the marks are part of the manufacturing process.

The initial issue of 1795-1804 was widely melted and exported because it was undervalued relative to its gold content, particularly by European standards. As a result, eagle production was suspended for more than 30 years.

Production resumed in 1838 on the reduced gold standard adopted in 1834 to prevent these abuses. The new coin featured a Liberty head wearing a coronet, which was Christian Gobrecht's interpretation of a painting of Venus by Benjamin West. A new, more realistic reverse eagle still wore a heraldic shield. This design continued until 1907. The motto "In God We Trust" was added to the reverse above the eagle in 1866.

In 1908, as part of the same coin design beautification trend that later introduced the Walking Liberty half dollar and Mercury dime, President Theodore Roosevelt asked noted sculptor Augustus Saint-Gaudens to prepare new designs for the eagle and double eagle. His work showed the head of Liberty wearing an Indian war bonnet. The headdress was added to Saint-Gaudens' original design at the president's instruction. The reverse featured a proud eagle with closed wings.

Saint-Gaudens' design originally did not include the motto "In God We Trust" because Roosevelt considered its use on coins sacrilegious, but Congress passed a law mandating that it be added in 1908.

The generic term "eagle" for the denomination of a gold $10 coin should be not be confused with the official term American Eagle bullion coins used to described the U.S. Mint's current silver and gold issues produced as a convenient way for individuals to own precious metals.

Known Counterfeits: 1799, 1858 (altered), 1889 (altered from Ps), 1901S, 1906D, 1906S, 1907, 1908 with-motto Proof,

1908S, 1909 Matte Proof, 1909S, 1910 Proof, 1910S, 1911 Proof, 1911D, 1911S, 1912S, 1913, 1913S, 1914S, 1915S, 1916S, 1926, 1932, 1933, among others, especially 1870 to 1933. Be cautious of false "C" mintmarks made by cutting down an authentic "O" mintmark. Beware of traces of solder on earlier coins used as jewelry. Look for interruption in the pattern of edge reeding. Be cautious of cleaned coins, which are harder to detect on gold because it usually does not tone naturally.

Coronet	VF	XF
1838, old-style head	2,650.00	6,850.00
1839, old-style head, large letters	1,150.00	2,150.00
1839, small letters	1,550.00	6,850.00
1840	515.00	650.00
1841	500.00	600.00
1841O	3,450.00	6,950.00
1842, small date	500.00	585.00
1842, large date	500.00	575.00
1842O	515.00	890.00
1843	500.00	690.00
1843O	515.00	645.00
1844	1,350.00	3,200.00
1844O	515.00	830.00
1845	675.00	770.00

Coronet	VF	XF
1845O	515.00	875.00
1846	745.00	1,250.00
1846O	515.00	1,150.00
1847	500.00	520.00
1847O	500.00	520.00
1848	500.00	585.00
1848O	695.00	1,850.00
1849	500.00	520.00
1849O	695.00	2,450.00
1850, large date	500.00	520.00
1850, small date	695.00	1,150.00
1850O	530.00	1,275.00
1851	500.00	520.00
1851O	515.00	575.00
1852	500.00	520.00
1852O	675.00	1,650.00
1853, 3 over 2	530.00	855.00
1853	515.00	520.00
1853O	530.00	585.00
1854	500.00	545.00
1854O, small date	530.00	825.00
1854O, large date	670.00	925.00

18490 Gold $10 with Coronet (No Motto)

Coronet	VF	XF
1854S	500.00	545.00
1855	500.00	520.00
1855O	530.00	2,100.00
1855S	1,950.00	3,250.00
1856	500.00	520.00
1856O	830.00	2,150.00
1856S	500.00	595.00
1857	530.00	1,050.00
1857O	1,800.00	3,650.00
1857S	515.00	1,050.00
1858	5,200.00	8,250.00
1858O	500.00	845.00
1858S	1,600.00	3,950.00
1859	530.00	700.00
1859O	4,250.00	10,500.00
1859S	2,600.00	5,250.00
1860	570.00	755.00
1860O	670.00	1,850.00
1860S	2,950.00	6,400.00
1861	500.00	520.00
1861S	1,600.00	3,750.00
1862	660.00	1,200.00

1862S Gold $10 with Coronet (No Motto)

Coronet	VF	XF
1862S	2,000.00	3,450.00
1863	4,000.00	10,000.00
1863S	1,600.00	3,750.00
1864	1,800.00	4,950.00
1864S	5,100.00	17,500.00
1865	1,950.00	4,850.00
1865S	4,850.00	12,500.00
1865S, 865 over inverted 186	3,450.00	8,750.00
1866S, no motto above ealge	2,650.00	5,950.00

Coronet, Motto Above Eagle	VF	XF
1866	850.00	2,450.00
1866S	1,550.00	3,850.00
1867	1,500.00	2,600.00
1867S	2,350.00	6,650.00
1868	550.00	1,100.00
1868S	1,350.00	2,400.00
1869	1,550.00	3,000.00
1869S	1,500.00	2,700.00
1870	985.00	1,650.00
1870CC	13,000.00	30,000.00
1870S	1,150.00	2,850.00
1871	1,500.00	3,000.00

Coronet, Motto Above Eagle	VF	XF
1871CC	2,600.00	6,400.00
1871S	1,300.00	2,200.00
1872	2,400.00	5,500.00
1872CC	2,850.00	9,850.00
1872S	675.00	1,175.00
1873	4,500.00	9,750.00
1873CC	6,000.00	13,500.00
1873S	1,150.00	2,850.00
1874	500.00	515.00
1874CC	1,150.00	3,650.00
1874S	1,275.00	3,400.00
1875	40,000.00	67,500.00
1875CC	4,250.00	9,850.00
1876	3,000.00	8,500.00
1876CC	3,600.00	7,750.00
1876S	1,300.00	2,950.00
1877	3,350.00	6,350.00
1877CC	2,400.00	6,750.00
1877S	550.00	1,250.00
1878	485.00	515.00
1878CC	3,850.00	10,000.00
1878S	525.00	775.00
1879	490.00	515.00

1873CC Gold $10 with Coronet and Motto

Coronet, Motto Above Eagle	VF	XF
1879CC	6,650.00	12,500.00
1879O	2,150.00	5,450.00
1879S	490.00	515.00
1880	470.00	480.00
1880CC	625.00	1,000.00
1880O	590.00	1,450.00
1880S	470.00	480.00
1881	470.00	480.00
1881CC	670.00	825.00
1881O	570.00	865.00
1881S	470.00	480.00
1882	470.00	480.00
1882CC	985.00	1,750.00
1882O	500.00	665.00
1882S	500.00	515.00
1883	470.00	480.00
1883CC	670.00	1,250.00
1883O	3,000.00	7,950.00
1883S	500.00	515.00
1884	500.00	515.00
1884CC	690.00	1,450.00
1884S	470.00	480.00
1885	470.00	480.00

18820 Gold $10 with Coronet and Motto

Coronet, Motto Above Eagle	VF	XF
1885S	470.00	480.00
1886	470.00	480.00
1886S	470.00	480.00
1887	500.00	515.00
1887S	470.00	480.00
1888	500.00	515.00
1888O	500.00	515.00
1888S	470.00	480.00
1889	530.00	700.00
1889S	470.00	480.00
1890	510.00	535.00
1890CC	610.00	700.00
1891	530.00	555.00
1891CC	610.00	660.00
1892	470.00	480.00
1892CC	610.00	660.00
1892O	500.00	515.00
1892S	500.00	540.00
1893	470.00	480.00
1893CC	610.00	700.00
1893O	500.00	515.00
1893S	500.00	515.00
1894	470.00	480.00

Coronet, Motto Above Eagle	VF	XF
1894O	500.00	515.00
1894S	500.00	540.00
1895	470.00	480.00
1895O	500.00	515.00
1895S	500.00	530.00
1896	470.00	480.00
1896S	500.00	510.00
1897	470.00	480.00
1897O	500.00	515.00
1897S	500.00	510.00
1898	470.00	480.00
1898S	500.00	510.00
1899	470.00	480.00
1899O	500.00	515.00
1899S	470.00	480.00
1900	470.00	480.00
1900S	500.00	515.00
1901	470.00	480.00
1901O	500.00	515.00
1901S	470.00	480.00
1902	470.00	480.00
1902S	470.00	480.00
1903	470.00	480.00

1901 Gold $10 with Coronet and Motto

Coronet, Motto Above Eagle	VF	XF
1903O	500.00	515.00
1903S	470.00	480.00
1904	470.00	480.00
1904O	500.00	515.00
1905	470.00	480.00
1905S	500.00	510.00
1906	470.00	480.00
1906D	470.00	480.00
1906O	500.00	515.00
1906S	500.00	510.00
1907	470.00	480.00
1907D	470.00	480.00
1907S	500.00	510.00

Indian Head, No Motto on Reverse	VF	XF
1907, wire rim, periods	9,500.00	14,900.00
1907, rounded rim, periods	26,000.00	38,500.00
1907, no periods	580.00	600.00
1908	565.00	585.00
1908D	565.00	585.00

Indian Head, With Motto on Reverse	VF	XF
1908S	575.00	635.00
1909	560.00	580.00

1907 Gold $10 with Indian Head and No Motto

Indian Head, With Motto on Reverse	VF	XF
1909D	565.00	585.00
1909S	565.00	585.00
1910	560.00	580.00
1910D	555.00	575.00
1910S	565.00	585.00
1911	555.00	575.00
1911D	610.00	675.00
1911S	500.00	555.00
1912	560.00	580.00
1912S	565.00	585.00
1913	560.00	580.00
1913S	610.00	650.00
1914	560.00	580.00
1914D	560.00	580.00
1914S	570.00	590.00
1915	560.00	580.00
1915S	610.00	725.00
1916S	600.00	615.00
1920S	7,800.00	11,000.00
1926	555.00	575.00
1930S	7,500.00	10,000.00
1932	555.00	575.00
1933	110,000.00	140,000.00

1913 Gold $10 with Indian Head and Motto

FIRST SPOUSES (GOLD $10)

Issued in conjunction with the circulating Presidential dollars, this series of gold $10 pieces depicts the First Lady of each presidency. The Jefferson, Jackson, and Van Buren administration's coin depicts Liberty, as there was no First Lady during their years in office.

First Spouses	MS-63	PF-65
2007W, Martha Washington	600.00	600.00
2007W, Abigail Adams	600.00	600.00
2007W, Liberty (Jefferson)	600.00	600.00
2007W, Dolley Madison	600.00	600.00
2008W, Elizabeth Monroe	600.00	600.00
2008W, Louisa Adams	600.00	600.00
2008W, Liberty (Jackson)	600.00	600.00
2008W, Liberty (Van Buren)	600.00	600.00

Martha Washington and Abigail Adams

Liberty (Jefferson) and Dolley Madison

Elizabeth Monroe and Louisa Adams

Liberty (Jackson) and Liberty (Van Buren)

DOUBLE EAGLES (GOLD $20)

The California Gold Rush of the 1840s resulted in large quantities of precious metal being presented at U.S. Mint facilities for coinage. To process the bullion more expediently, and because of the obvious convenience of using fewer coins for large international payments, the bill proposing the introduction of gold dollars was amended to include a gold $20 piece, to be called a "double eagle." Designer James B. Longacre engraved a bust of Liberty wearing a coronet similar to the one used on smaller gold coins since 1838 but of a much more refined style. A facing heraldic eagle with a circlet of stars and a radiant arc above graced the reverse. The two motto ribbons at its sides suggested the denomination of two eagles.

This basic design continued until 1907. In 1861 the reverse was redesigned subtly by Anthony C. Paquet, but it was withdrawn soon after its release. In 1866 the motto "In God We Trust" was added on the reverse above the eagle. In 1877 the inscription "Twenty D." on the reverse was replaced with "Twenty Dollars."

In 1908, as part of the same coin design beautification trend that later introduced the Walking Liberty half dollar and Mercury dime, President Theodore Roosevelt asked noted sculptor Augustus Saint-Gaudens to prepare new designs for the double eagle and eagle. His work showed a full figure of

Liberty holding a torch and olive branch and striding toward the viewer. It was inspired by Hellenistic sculpture, as correspondence between the president and sculptor reveals. The reverse featured an eagle in mid-flight with a rising sun and rays in the background.

In the coin's first year of production, its high relief was lowered because it required three strikes by the coining press to bring it up. Also, the Roman numerals used in the date were changed to more conventional Arabic numerals. Saint-Gaudens' design originally did not include the motto "In God We Trust" because Roosevelt considered its use on coins sacrilegious, but Congress passed a law mandating that it be added in 1908.

Liberty and Saint-Gaudens double eagles are often found with heavy bag marks because of their soft metal and heavy weight. Examples virtually free from these marks command a substantial premium.

Known Counterfeits: 1879, 1879O, 1881 (altered), 1882 (altered), 1887 (altered), 1891, 1894, 1897S, 1898S, 1899S, 1900, 1900S, 1901S, 1903, 1903S, 1904, 1904S, 1906, 1906S, MCMVII, 1907 (Saint-Gaudens), 1908, 1909, 1910D, 1910S, 1911D, 1914D, 1914S, 1915, 1916S, 1919, 1920, 1921, 1922, 1923, 1924, 1925, 1926, 1927, 1927D (altered), 1928, 1929, among others, especially 1870 to 1932. Beware of traces of solder on earlier coins used as jewelry. Look for interruption in the pattern of edge reeding. Be cautious of cleaned coins, which are harder to detect in gold because it does not tone naturally.

Liberty, "Twenty D.," No Motto Above Eagle	VF	XF
1849, unique, Smithsonian collection	—	—
1850	1,235.00	1,325.00
1850O	1,250.00	2,000.00
1851	1,275.00	1,350.00
1851O	1,100.00	1,650.00
1852	1,275.00	1,350.00
1852O	1,250.00	2,100.00
1853, 3 over 2	1,355.00	1,550.00
1853	1,275.00	875.00
1853O	1,365.00	2,850.00
1854	1,275.00	1,350.00
1854O	95,000.00	175,000.00
1854S	1,250.00	1,325.00
1855	1,275.00	1,350.00
1855O	3,650.00	14,000.00
1855S	1,250.00	1,350.00
1856	1,275.00	1,350.00
1856O	97,500.00	140,000.00
1856S	1,250.00	1,350.00
1857	1,275.00	1,350.00

1850 Gold $20 with Liberty Head

Liberty, "Twenty D.," No Motto Above Eagle	VF	XF
1857O	1,300.00	2,250.00
1857S	1,250.00	1,350.00
1858	1,330.00	1,370.00
1858O	1,950.00	2,900.00
1858S	1,250.00	1,370.00
1859	1,325.00	1,850.00
1859O	6,400.00	10,000.00
1859S	1,250.00	1,350.00
1860	1,250.00	1,350.00
1860O	3,650.00	9,500.00
1860S	1,275.00	1,380.00
1861	1,250.00	1,350.00
1861O, Most struck by Louisiana and the Confederacy after withdrawal from the Union.	5,650.00	13,650.00
1861S	1,275.00	1,380.00
1861, Paquet reverse, two known		Novermber 1988 auction, $660,000.00
1861S, Paquet reverse	19,500.00	52,500.00
1862	1,250.00	2,250.00
1862S	1,240.00	1,350.00
1863	1,250.00	1,900.00
1863S	1,240.00	1,350.00

Liberty, "Twenty D.," No Motto Above Eagle	VF	XF
1864	1,250.00	1,350.00
1864S	1,240.00	1,350.00
1865	1,250.00	1,350.00
1865S	1,240.00	1,340.00
1866S	3,400.00	13,500.00

Liberty, "Twenty D.,"Motto Above Eagle	VF	XF
1866	1,170.00	1,310.00
1866S	1,170.00	1,320.00
1867	1,170.00	1,325.00
1867S	1,170.00	1,320.00
1868	1,210.00	1,250.00
1868S	1,170.00	1,290.00
1869	1,180.00	1,375.00
1869S	1,170.00	1,310.00
1870	1,190.00	1,340.00
1870CC	125,000.00	195,000.00
1870S	1,170.00	1,310.00
1871	1,180.00	1,310.00
1871CC	9,500.00	19,500.00
1871S	1,170.00	1,280.00
1872	1,170.00	1,310.00
1872CC	2,450.00	5,450.00
1872S	1,170.00	1,310.00

1869S Gold $20 with Liberty Head

Liberty, "Twenty D.,"Motto Above Eagle	VF	XF
1873, closed 3	1,170.00	1,370.00
1873, open 3	1,170.00	1,310.00
1873CC	2,900.00	4,750.00
1873S	1,170.00	1,280.00
1874	1,170.00	1,310.00
1874CC	1,400.00	1,950.00
1874S	1,170.00	1,280.00
1875	1,170.00	1,310.00
1875CC	1,300.00	1,550.00
1875S	1,170.00	1,280.00
1876	1,170.00	1,300.00
1876CC	1,300.00	1,500.00
1876S	1,170.00	1,280.00

Liberty Head, "Twenty Dollars," Motto Above Eagle	VF	XF
1877	1,000.00	1,145.00
1877CC	1,500.00	1,900.00
1877S	1,000.00	1,050.00
1878	1,020.00	1,145.00
1878CC	2,450.00	3,950.00
1878S	1,000.00	1,020.00
1879	1,080.00	1,150.00
1879CC	3,000.00	4,850.00

1877 Gold $20 with Liberty Head

Liberty Head, "Twenty Dollars," Motto Above Eagle	VF	XF
1879O	12,500.00	21,500.00
1879S	1,000.00	1,020.00
1880	1,110.00	1,175.00
1880S	1,000.00	1,020.00
1881	6,800.00	12,500.00
1881S	1,000.00	1,020.00
1882	11,500.00	29,500.00
1882CC	1,350.00	1,750.00
1882S	1,000.00	1,020.00
1883, proof	—	14,000.00
1883CC	1,350.00	1,600.00
1883S	1,000.00	1,020.00
1884, proof	—	15,000.00
1884CC	1,250.00	1,550.00
1884S	1,000.00	1,020.00
1885	8,800.00	13,850.00
1885CC	2,500.00	3,850.00
1885S	1,000.00	1,020.00
1886	12,500.00	29,500.00
1887, proof	—	26,500.00
1887S	1,000.00	1,020.00
1888	1,000.00	1,020.00

Liberty Head, "Twenty Dollars," Motto Above Eagle	VF	XF
1888S	1,000.00	1,020.00
1889	1,160.00	1,275.00
1889CC	1,500.00	1,750.00
1889S	1,000.00	1,020.00
1890	1,000.00	1,050.00
1890CC	1,250.00	1,450.00
1890S	1,000.00	1,020.00
1891	3,500.00	5,750.00
1891CC	4,800.00	9,000.00
1891S	1,000.00	1,020.00
1892	1,350.00	2,250.00
1892CC	1,350.00	1,750.00
1892S	1,000.00	1,020.00
1893	1,000.00	1,040.00
1893CC	1,550.00	1,900.00
1893S	960.00	975.00
1894	960.00	975.00
1894S	960.00	975.00
1895	960.00	975.00
1895S	960.00	975.00
1896	960.00	975.00
1896S	960.00	975.00

Liberty Head, "Twenty Dollars," Motto Above Eagle	VF	XF
1897	960.00	975.00
1897S	960.00	975.00
1898	965.00	1,000.00
1898S	965.00	975.00
1899	960.00	975.00
1899S	960.00	975.00
1900	960.00	975.00
1900S	960.00	975.00
1901	960.00	975.00
1901S	960.00	975.00
1902	960.00	1,170.00
1902S	960.00	975.00
1903	960.00	975.00
1903S	960.00	975.00
1904	960.00	975.00
1904S	960.00	975.00
1905	965.00	995.00
1905S	960.00	975.00
1906	965.00	980.00
1906D	960.00	975.00
1906S	960.00	975.00
1907	960.00	975.00

1903 Gold $20 with Liberty Head

Liberty Head, "Twenty Dollars," Motto Above Eagle	VF	XF
1907D	960.00	975.00
1907S	960.00	975.00

Saint-Gaudens, No Motto Below Eagle	VF	XF
1907, high relief, wire rim	7,500.00	8,350.00
1907, high relief, flat rim	7,750.00	8,850.00
1907, Arabic numerals	1,020.00	1,030.00
1908	1,010.00	1,020.00
1908D	1,020.00	1,030.00

Saint-Gaudens, Motto Below Eagle	VF	XF
1908	1,015.00	1,025.00
1908D	1,020.00	1,030.00
1908S	2,450.00	3,150.00
1909/8	1,020.00	1,030.00
1909	1,030.00	1,050.00
1909D	1,060.00	1,070.00
1909S	1,020.00	1,030.00
1910	1,015.00	1,025.00
1910D	1,015.00	1,025.00
1910S	1,020.00	1,030.00
1911	1,020.00	1,030.00
1911D	1,015.00	1,025.00

1907 High Relief Saint-Gaudens Gold $20 with No Motto

1909 Saint-Gaudens Gold $20 with Motto

Saint-Gaudens, Motto Below Eagle	VF	XF
1911S	1,015.00	1,025.00
1912	1,020.00	1,030.00
1913	1,020.00	1,030.00
1913D	1,015.00	1,025.00
1913S	1,070.00	1,080.00
1914	1,030.00	1,040.00
1914D	1,015.00	1,025.00
1914S	1,015.00	1,025.00
1915	1,020.00	1,030.00
1915S	1,015.00	1,025.00
1916S	1,020.00	1,030.00
1920	1,010.00	1,020.00
1920S	14,500.00	18,500.00
1921	35,000.00	43,500.00
1922	1,010.00	1,020.00
1922S	1,130.00	1,150.00
1923	1,010.00	1,020.00
1923D	1,020.00	1,030.00
1924	1,010.00	1,020.00
1924D	1,235.00	1,550.00
1924S	1,130.00	1,550.00
1925	1,010.00	1,020.00
1925D	1,550.00	2,100.00

Saint-Gaudens, Motto Below Eagle	VF	XF
1925S	1,350.00	1,950.00
1926	1,010.00	1,020.00
1926D	10,000.00	15,500.00
1926S	1,210.00	1,550.00
1927	1,010.00	1,020.00
1927D	155,000.00	200,000.00
1927S	6,850.00	8,850.00
1928	1,010.00	1,020.00
1929	6,950.00	8,450.00
1930S	35,000.00	41,000.00
1931	10,500.00	13,500.00
1931D	8,850.00	11,500.00
1932	12,500.00	14,500.00
1933, 13 known	—	9,000,000.00

MODERN COMMEMORATIVES

The first U.S. commemorative coin was an 1892 half dollar for the Columbian Exposition. The Columbian half dollar opened the door to many other commemorative coins from the 1910s and continuing into the 1950s. Most were silver half dollars, but there was also an 1893 quarter (also for the Columbian Exposition), a number of gold dollars, two gold $2.50 coins, and two gold $50 coins.

The coins were sold by the Mint at a premium above face value with a portion of the proceeds benefiting some organization or event related to the coin's theme. Some of the coins commemorated state anniversaries or national themes, such as the U.S. Sesquicentennial in 1926.

There were no less than 18 commemorative half dollars issued in 1936 alone. Among them was an issue commemorating the 75th anniversary of the Battle of Gettysburg. Others, however, were of little national importance, such as issues for the Cincinnati Music Center and the centennial of Elgin, Ill.

Congress grew weary of U.S. coinage being used as local fundraisers, and the flow of commemorative coins slowed in the 1940s and '50s. The last issue among what are commonly called "early" commemoratives was a 1954 half dollar honoring Booker T. Washington and George Washington Carver.

A 28-year hiatus on commemorative coinage ensued until Congress authorized a half dollar in the traditional 90-percent-silver composition to honor the 250th anniversary of George Washington's birth in 1982. Thus began what are commonly called "modern" commemoratives.

Like the Columbian half dollar 90 years earlier, the George Washington half dollar opened the door to more commemorative coinage, and like the commemorative coinage of the 1930s, an undesirable proliferation resulted. The coins' themes in the 1990s weren't as localized as many of those in the 1930s, but commemorative coinage became an easy mark for U.S. senators and representatives looking to do a favor for a constituency or a favor for a fellow lawmaker by offering their vote for a commemorative coin program. Commemorative coins could raise funds for a pet cause through surcharges on the Mint's sales of the coins, and a vote for a program went largely unnoticed by the general public.

The year 1994 alone brought five commemorative coin programs.

In response, Congress passed the Commemorative Coin Reform Act of 1996. Among other provisions, it limits the number of commemorative themes to two per year. In addition, congressional proposals for commemorative coins must be reviewed by the Citizens Coinage Advisory Committee, which reports to the U.S. Treasury secretary. The 10-person committee consists of members from the general public and those with credentials in American history, sculpture, and numismatics.

Some of the least popular commemorative coins at the time of their issue are the most expensive on the secondary market today, and some of the most popular commemorative coins at the time of their issue are the most affordable today. The least popular coins didn't sell as well, which resulted in lower mintages. The scarcer coins generally are more valued by collectors, which increases demand and drives up their asking prices on the secondary market.

Silver Half Dollars	MS-65	PF-65
1982 George Washington, 250th Anniversary of Birth	6.50	6.50
1993 James Madison, Father of the Bill of Rights	20.00	16.50

Clad Half Dollars	MS-65	PF-65
1986 Statue of Liberty Centennial	5.50	5.50
1986 Bicentennial of Congress	8.00	8.00
1991 Mount Rushmore Golden Anniversary	21.50	20.00
1991 World War II 50th Anniversary (struck in 1993)	29.00	26.50
1992 Olympics	8.50	8.50
1992 500th Anniversary of Columbus Discovery	11.50	11.50
1994 World Cup Soccer	10.00	8.50
1995 Atlanta Olympics, basketball design	22.50	18.00

1986S Half-Dollar Commemorative Statue of Liberty Centennial

1992S Half-Dollar Commemorative Olympics

Clad Half Dollars	MS-65	PF-65
1995 Atlanta Olympics, baseball design	22.50	19.00
1995 Civil War	42.50	41.50
1996 Atlanta Olympics, soccer design	110.00	105.00
1996 Atlanta Olympics, swimmer design	165.00	36.00
2001 U.S. Capitol	13.50	17.50
2003 First Flight Centennial	15.50	15.50
2008 Bald Eagle	—	—
Silver Dollars	MS-65	PF-65
1983 Los Angeles XXII Olympiad	14.00	14.00
1983 Los Angeles XXII Olympiad	14.50	14.00
1986 Statue of Liberty Centennial	14.00	14.00
1987 The U.S. Constitution 200th Anniversary	14.00	14.00

Silver Dollars	MS-65	PF-65
1988 Olympiad	14.00	14.00
1989 Bicentennial of the Congress	16.50	18.50
1990 Eisenhower Centennial	15.00	17.00
1991 38th Anniversary of Korean War	16.50	20.00
1991 Mount Rushmore Golden Anniversary	32.00	30.00
1991 USO 50th Anniversary	14.00	19.50
1991-1995 World War II 50th Anniversary (struck in 1993)	30.00	40.00
1992 Columbus Quincentenary	30.00	40.00
1992 Olympics	25.00	26.00
1992 The White House, 1792-1992	30.00	30.00
1993 James Madison	19.50	20.00
1993 Thomas Jefferson, 1743-1993	23.00	28.00
1994 National Prisoner of War Museum	90.00	45.00
1994 Bicentennial of United States Capitol	20.00	25.00
1994 Vietnam Veterans Memorial	85.00	70.00
1994 Women in Military Service Memorial	40.00	35.00
1994 World Cup '94	25.00	30.00
1995 Atlanta Olympics, gymnastics design	75.00	60.00
1995 Atlanta Olympics, track and field design	100.00	55.00
1995 Atlanta Olympics, cycling design	150.00	50.00
1995 Atlanta Olympics, Paralympics design	95.00	65.00
1995 Civil War	75.00	80.00
1995 Special Olympics, World Games	30.00	25.00

1995S Silver-Dollar Commemorative Civil War

Silver Dollars	MS-65	PF-65
1996 Atlanta Olympics, tennis design	330.00	90.00
1996 Atlanta Olympics, rowing design	345.00	75.00
1996 Atlanta Olympics, high-jumper design	400.00	60.00
1996 Atlanta Olympics, Paralympics design	385.00	90.00
1996 National Community Service	235.00	80.00
1996 Smithsonian Institution, 1846-1996	150.00	70.00
1997 Jackie Robinson, 50th Anniversary	100.00	85.00
1997 National Law Enforcement Officers Memorial	165.00	135.00
1997 United States Botanic Garden, 1820-1995	45.00	45.00
1998 Black Revolutionary War Patriots	175.00	125.00
1998 Robert F. Kennedy	35.00	45.00
1999 Dolley Madison	50.00	50.00
1999 Yellowstone National Park	55.00	60.00
2000 Leif Ericson	90.00	70.00
2000 Library of Congress, 1800-2000	45.00	40.00
2001 American Buffalo	260.00	290.00
2001 U.S. Capitol, 1800-2001	35.00	45.00
2002 West Point Bicentennial	20.00	19.50
2002 XIX Olympic Winter Games	35.00	40.00
2003 First Flight Centennial	35.00	30.00
2004 125th Anniversary of the Light Bulb	40.00	40.00
2004 Lewis & Clark Bicentennial	35.00	30.00
2005 Chief Justice John Marshall	35.00	40.00
2005 Marines, 1775-2005	45.00	55.00

1997S Silver-Dollar Commemorative Jackie Robinson, 50th Anniversary

2004P Silver-Dollar Commemorative 125th Anniversary of the Light Bulb

Silver Dollars	MS-65	PF-65
2006 Benjamin Franklin Tercentenary, portrait design	50.00	55.00
2006 Benjamin Franklin Tercentenary, kite-flying design	50.00	55.00
2006 San Francisco Old Mint	50.00	45.00
2007 Founding of Jamestown, 1607-2007	50.00	55.00
2007 Little Rock High School Desegregation	50.00	50.00
2008 Bald Eagle	50.00	—

Gold $5	MS-65	PF-65
1986 Statue of Liberty Centennial	225.00	225.00
1987 Bicentennial of the Constitution	225.00	225.00
1988 Olympiad	225.00	225.00
1989 Bicentennial of the Congress	225.00	225.00
1991 Mount Rushmore Golden Anniversary	285.00	225.00
1991-1995 World War II 50th Anniversary (struck in 1993)	360.00	330.00
1992 Columbus Quincentenary	320.00	285.00
1993 James Madison	325.00	265.00
1994 World Cup '94	325.00	265.00
1995 Civil War	900.00	535.00
1995 Atlanta Olympics, torch-runner design	775.00	410.00
1995 Atlanta Olympics, stadium design	1,200.00	535.00
1996 Atlanta Olympics, cauldron design	1,000.00	600.00
1996 Atlanta Olympics, flag-bearer design	1,050.00	615.00

Gold $5	MS-65	PF-65
1996 Smithsonian Institution, 1846-1996	1,500.00	720.00
1997 Franklin Delano Roosevelt	1,100.00	565.00
1997 Jackie Robinson 50th Anniversary	5,750.00	900.00
1999 George Washington, bicentennial of death	475.00	475.00
2001 U.S. Capitol, 1801-2000	2,150.00	465.00
2002 XIX Olympic Winter Games	550.00	510.00
2006 San Francisco Old Mint	285.00	—
2007 Foudning of Jamestown, 1607-2007	285.00	275.00
2008 Bald Eagle	285.00	—

Gold $10	MS-65	PF-65
1984 Los Angeles XXII Olympiad	450.00	450.00
2000 Library of Congress	3,600.00	1,350.00
2003 First Flight Centennial	625.00	560.00

2003W Gold $10 Commemorative First Flight Centennial

U.S. PROOF SETS

Proof coins originated centuries ago when specially produced pieces were prepared as examples of the ideal coin, often for reference or royal approval. U.S. proof coins are known from at least the early 1800s, but they were not widely available. They were struck for VIPs and coin collectors and dealers with connections at the U.S. Mint.

As proof coins developed through the late 19th and early 20th centuries, certain criteria began to characterize their manufacture. Today, they typically are struck twice with highly polished dies on carefully prepared and polished blanks. Early in the 20th century, the dies were given a matte or sandblasted finish, but this soon fell out of favor. Recently, some proofs have been struck with a combination of finishes: a dull matte finish on the motifs, such as portraits, with a highly reflective, mirror-like surface in the fields. These are called cameo proofs and are more desirable than conventional proofs, which have a mirror-like finish over the entire surface.

In 1936, the Mint began selling proof sets to the general public. Each set usually contains one example of each circulating denomination. Proof sets have been offered in most years since their inception. Exceptions are 1943-1949 and 1965-1967. Proof sets of the 1950s were originally sold in cardboard boxes and then later in flat cellophane sheets inside a special envelope. Today, they come in hard-plastic cases. Proof sets not in their original holders usually trade at a discount. Such removal can damage their fragile surfaces by exposure to breath and humidity. Such maltreatment can cause "carbon spots," which is what collectors call the tiny black spots.

The Mint also offers proof versions of current commemoratives. They are marketed in sets with other commemoratives and also have been offered in sets with proof examples of currently circulating coins, called Prestige Sets. Congress has also authorized the striking of some proof coins in traditional 90-percent-silver composition.

Known Counterfeits: Proof sets are not generally counterfeited, but regular coins are occasionally altered to look like matte proofs.

1936	7,500.00
1937	4,350.00
1938	1,900.00
1939	1,800.00
1940	1,475.00
1941	1,450.00
1942, five coins	1,375.00
1942, six coins	1,475.00
1950	690.00

1951	565.00
1952	285.00
1953	250.00
1954	110.00
1955, box	115.00
1955, flat pack	165.00
1956	70.00
1957	30.00
1958	55.00
1959	30.00
1960, with large-date cent	23.00
1960, with small-date cent	35.00
1961	15.00
1962	15.00
1963	15.00
1964	16.00
1968S	7.50
1968S, with no-mintmark dime	17,500.00
1969S	7.00
1970S, with large-date cent	10.00
1970S, with small-date cent	100.00
1970S, with no-mintmark dime	1,350.00
1971S	4.50

1971S, with no-mintmark nickel	1,850.00
1972S	4.75
1973S	9.25
1974S	11.00
1975S	12.00
1975S, with no-mintmark dime	50,000.00
1976S	10.00
1976S, three coins, silver	17.00
1977S	8.50
1978S	9.50
1979S, type I	8.50
1979S, type II	120.00
1980S	8.50
1981S, type I	8.00
1981S, type II	400.00
1982S	4.75
1983S	7.00
1983S, with no-mintmark dime	1,050.00
1983S, Prestige Set	90.00
1984S	6.00
1984S, Prestige Set	25.00
1985S	5.75
1986S	8.50
1986S, Prestige Set	30.00

1987S	6.25
1987S, Prestige Set	23.00
1988S	7.00
1988S, Prestige Set	30.00
1989S	7.00
1989S, Prestige Set	40.00
1990S	8.00
1990S, with no-mintmark cent	6,650.00
1990S, Prestige Set	25.00
1990S, Prestige Set, with no-mintmark cent	7,000.00
1991S	12.50
1991S Prestige Set	60.00
1992S	7.25
1992S Prestige Set	70.00
1992S, silver	16.50
1992S, Premier Set	16.50
1993S	12.50
1993S, Prestige Set	35.00
1993S, silver	35.00
1993S, Silver Premier	35.00
1994S	12.50
1994S, Prestige Set	40.00
1994S, silver	40.00
1994S, Premier Set	40.00

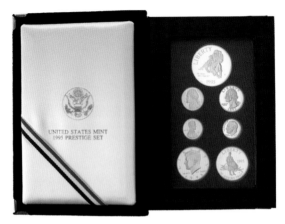

1995S Prestige Set

1995S	35.00
1995S, Prestige Set	130.00
1995S, silver	90.00
1995S, Premier Set	130.00
1996S	15.00
1996S, Prestige Set	475.00
1996S, silver	40.00
1996S, Premier Set	40.00
1997S	30.00

1997S, Prestige Set	160.00
1997S, silver	60.00
1997S, Premier Set	60.00
1998S	20.00
1998S, silver	30.00
1998, Premier Set	30.00
1999S	65.00
1999S, silver	330.00
1999, quarters	50.00
2000S	16.50
2000S, silver	30.00
2000S, quarters	10.00
2001S	100.00
2001S, silver	150.00
2001S, quarters	50.00
2002S	30.00
2002S, silver	60.00
2002S, quarters	20.00
2003S	22.00
2003S, silver	30.00
2003S, quarters	13.50
2004S	35.00
2004S, silver	30.00
2004S, quarters	18.00

1999 Proof Sets

2004S, silver quarters	21.00
2005S, quarters	12.50
2005S, silver quarters	20.00
2006S, quarters	13.00
2006S, silver quarters	22.00
2007S, quarters	15.50
2007S, silver quarters	25.00
2008S, quarters	15.50
2008S, silver quarters	25.00

U.S. MINT SETS

Coins in mint sets are struck using the same methods as those used for circulating coins, but they receive more careful handling at the mint. They allow collectors to obtain an uncirculated example of each coin struck for circulation that year.

Mint sets from 1947 to 1958 contain two examples of each coin. No traditional mint sets were produced from 1965 to 1967. Instead, the U.S. Mint offered "Special Mint Sets" of these years, which contained coins of superior quality (despite initial government claims to the contrary), perhaps to compensate for the lack of proof sets in those years.

The Philadelphia, Denver, and San Francisco mints all struck coins for circulation in those years, but no mintmarks were used, so their products cannot be distinguished. Sets made in 1966 and 1967 came in rigid plastic cases within a tight-fitting cardboard box. When mintmarks were resumed in 1968, the coins of the different mints were separated by placing them in blue or red plastic sleeves. Some recent mint sets also contain commemoratives. In 1982 and 1983, "Souvenir Sets" sold at the Mint replaced mint sets.

Mint sets must be in their original packaging to command a premium over loose, uncirculated coins. Removing mint-state coins from their protective packaging can damage them by exposing them to breath and humidity. Such maltreatment can cause "carbon spots" to form, much as they do on proof coins.

Known Counterfeits: When mint sets are offered in unofficial holders, be careful that a slightly circulated coin was not inserted in hopes of passing it off as uncirculated. Coins that originally constituted a mint set but were transferred to another holder will usually have matching toning typical of early sets. The plastic holders of 1966 and 1967 can easily be opened and other coins substituted.

1947	1,375.00
1948	750.00
1949	935.00
1950, none issued	—
1951	900.00
1952	825.00
1953	565.00
1954	265.00
1955	165.00
1956	165.00
1957	275.00
1958	150.00
1959	60.00
1960	30.00
1961	50.00
1962	28.00
1963	28.00
1964	28.00
1965, Special Mint Set	7.50
1966, Special Mint Set	7.25
1967, Special Mint Set	15.00
1968	6.00
1969	7.00
1970, with large-date cent	17.00

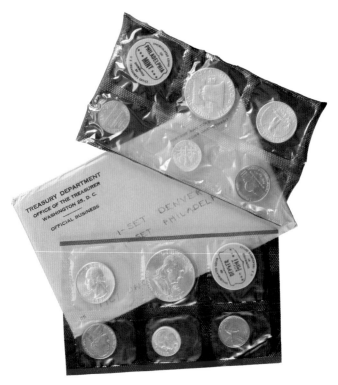

1961 Mint Set

1970, with small-date cent	70.00
1971	5.00
1972	5.00
1973	15.00
1974	6.00
1975	8.75
1976	10.00
1976S, three coins, silver	13.00
1977	8.00
1978	6.75
1979, This set is incomplete in that it lacks the Anthony dollar.	6.75
1980	7.25
1981	14.00
1982, none issued	—
1983, none issued	—
1984	6.75
1985	6.50
1986	13.50
1987	6.50
1988	6.25
1989	6.75
1990	7.50
1991	8.00
1992	7.50

1993	7.50
1994	6.75
1995	13.50
1996	23.00
1997	19.00
1998	6.75
1999	26.00
2000	10.00
2001	18.00
2002	15.00
2003	18.00
2004	60.00
2005	11.00
2006	16.00
2007	23.00
2008	—

2000D Mint Set

2002 One-Ounce Silver Walking Liberty Dollar

PAPER MONEY INTRODUCTION

The U.S. government did not issue paper money until the Civil War. During the Revolutionary War, the states and Continental Congress printed so much paper money to finance their expenses that its value evaporated and it became nearly worthless. As a result, when the Constitution was adopted, it specified, "No state shall ... make anything but gold and silver coin a tender in payment of debts." When the federal government finally did issue paper money, its use was limited. The first federal paper money, demand notes, even bore interest. Most federal paper money over the following century was redeemable in gold or silver.

There are many different types of U.S. paper money, as shown in the following sections. Their common names, usually found at the top of the note as a heading, and often the colors of their seals indicate the law that authorized their issue and the nature of their backing.

Almost all U.S. paper currency bears a date, but this is not necessarily the year it was actually printed. It is the year of the act authorizing the series or the year the series went into

Large-Size One-Dollar Silver Certificate, Series 1899

production. The signature combinations on bank notes can often be used to date them.

Originally paper money was larger than current issues. Until 1928, notes were about 7-1/2 inches by 3-1/8 inches. Beginning with Series 1928 (released in 1929), U.S. paper money changed to 6-1/8 inches by 2-5/8 inches. The fractional notes of the Civil War were smaller than current notes but varied in size.

GRADING PAPER MONEY

State of preservation is as important for paper money as it is for coins. Paper money is primarily graded to describe the amount of wear, but other factors can influence value. Many of the same grading terms used for coins are also used for paper money. Of course, the physical nature of paper requires a different set of definitions. They are briefly described here:

Crisp Uncirculated (CU)—A note that is as pristine as it was when issued. It is literally crisp, with sharply pointed corners. It must have absolutely no folds, tears, or edge rounding, and no stains or staple holes.

Extremely Fine (XF)—A particularly nice note with only the slightest signs of wear. It will still be crisp to the touch. Slight rounding of the corner points is possible, but there should be no significant folds or creases, tears, stains or staple holes.

A convenient method of detecting creases in a note is to hold it up to a narrow light source and look at it from an acute angle, though not directly in the direction of the light.

Very Fine (VF)—A nice, clean note with obvious but moderate signs of wear. Creases that break the ink will be visible but generally only one in each direction and neither too deep. Its corner points will be dull. Although not limp, it will have only some of the crispness of better-grade notes. No significant stains will be visible.

Fine (F)—A worn, but not worn-out note. It has no crispness left. It will have heavy creases, but none that threatens the structural integrity. Its edges may not be perfectly smooth but are not irregularly worn. Trivial ink marks and smudges are acceptable.

Very Good (VG)—A worn and limp note with serious, deep creases. The edges are worn and not even. Some ink marks or smudges are visible. Tiny tears may be present, but no parts are missing. Small staple or pin holes are acceptable.

Good (G)—This condition is not considered collectible for most purposes. Only the rarest of notes in this grade could find a home with most collectors. A note grading good is usually limp, heavily creased, stained, ripped, and pinned or stapled. Some of the creases will permit spots of light to shine through the note at their intersections.

HANDLING PAPER MONEY

Never fold paper money; it immediately reduces its value. When in doubt as to whether a note has value, place it flat in a book until you can consult an expert. Do not carry a note that may have value in your wallet. When handling a note, remember that its most fragile parts are its corners; never touch them. Also, never repair a tear in a note with tape. The tape usually is a greater detriment to the note's value than the tear. Attempts to clean a note are also likely to cause damage.

COUNTERFEIT PAPER MONEY

Detecting counterfeit notes is not as difficult or as mysterious as many presume, but many of the detection methods used by merchants are so inefficient they are of no value.

Since its beginning, U.S. paper money has been printed on cloth rather than paper. It is part cotton and part linen with some silk. The silk is in the form of minute red and blue threads, which dive in and out of the note's surface. A color copier may be able to reproduce the colors of these tiny threads, but it cannot reproduce the texture of threads entering and leaving the note's surface. Use a magnifying glass to look for texture.

Another key to detecting counterfeits is examining the crispness of the ink in the design. Images and lines should be sharp and distinct.

Minimal effort looking for these clues can catch most circulating counterfeits. Most counterfeit bills pass in circulation not because the counterfeits are deceptive but because little or no effort is made to determine if they are genuine.

In recent years, Federal Reserve notes have incorporated many new anti-counterfeiting devices to defeat high-tech reproductions. Occasionally, however, real notes have been used to create counterfeits. A counterfeiter will take the value numbers from the corners of a note and glue them to a note of a lower face value. Such notes will often feel too thick or irregular at the corners. Most important, the counterfeiter presumes the recipients will pay little attention to the notes they accept. Such counterfeits can be detected by even the quickest comparison with a real note.

Certain practices are designed to take an authentic note and make it appear to be in a better grade of preservation than it is. These include ironing a note to make it look less worn and expertly gluing tears. To detect these alterations, hold the note up to a light. Light will pass through the glue differently than it will through normal currency.

When choosing a paper-money dealer, make sure he or she has the skills to authenticate a note and the ethics to accept it back if it is not authentic. The International Bank Note Society and the Professional Currency Dealers Association enforce codes of ethics among their members.

DEMAND NOTES

The demand notes of 1861 were the first paper money issued by the U.S. government. They were put into circulation under the emergency circumstances of the Civil War. The bad experiences of the overproduction of paper money during the Revolutionary War were still remembered, so limits were set on the uses of these notes. They differed from modern currency mostly because they were not officially legal tender but rather were "receivable in payment for all public dues." That is to say they were not good for "all debts public and private." One could use them to pay taxes, but they did not have to be accepted in private transactions. Later, a law was passed requiring their acceptance for private payments also. Their name "demand notes" derives from the statement on their face, "The United States promises to pay to the bearer on demand."

There were, however, limits on how demand notes could be redeemed. These notes were issued at five cities and could be redeemed by the assistant treasurers in the individual note's specific city of issue.

Designs were uniform from city to city. The $5 note shows at left the statue of Columbia from the U.S. Capitol and at right a portrait of Alexander Hamilton. The $10 shows Abraham Lincoln (then in office) at left, an eagle centered, and an allegorical figure of art at right. The $20 depicts Liberty holding a sword and shield.

The nickname "greenback" for paper money began with these notes, which have a distinctive green back. Privately issued paper money circulating until then had blank backs.

There are two major varieties of demand notes, resulting from the government being ill prepared for the practical reality of hand-signing millions of notes. The original intent was that clerks would be able to sign them "for the" Treasury register and "for the" U.S. treasurer. The time it took to handwrite the words "for the" millions of times quickly became excessive, so the words were printed on later notes instead of handwritten. The earlier varieties, with "for the" handwritten, are worth more than the prices listed here.

High-grade notes in this series are rare.

Known Counterfeits: Examine detail, check to make sure notes are hand signed, and use reasonable caution.

	F	VF
$5 Boston	3,000.00	6,400.00
$5 Cincinnati, rare	—	—
$5 New York	2,750.00	5,000.00
$5 Philadelphia	3,300.00	11,750.00
$5 St. Louis	—	38,000.00
$10 Boston	7,750.00	22,000.00
$10 Cincinnati, rare	—	—
$10 New York	4,750.00	20,000.00

Philadelphia Five-Dollar Demand Note, Series 1861

	F	VF
$10 Philadelphia	3,750.00	19,000.00
$10 St. Louis, rare	—	—
$20 Boston	25,000.00	—
$20 Cincinnati, unique	—	—
$20 New York	—	87,500.00
$20 Philadelphia	—	75,000.00

TREASURY NOTES

These notes, designated "Treasury notes" by the titles on their face inscriptions, are also called "coin notes." This was because the Treasury secretary was required to redeem the notes in his choice of gold or silver coin, although the notes were backed by silver bullion rather than coin.

Treasury notes were issued only in 1890 and 1891. Both years have the same face designs, generally of military heroes. The original reverse designs featured the values spelled out in large letters. For 1891, they were redesigned to allow more blank space. The ornamentation of the two 0s in 100 on the reverse of the $100 notes is reminiscent of the pattern on the skin of a watermelon. Hence, they are known in the collecting community as "watermelon notes."

Known Counterfeits: Examine detail and silk threads in paper, and use reasonable caution.

	F	XF
$1 1890 Edwin M. Stanton	700.00	2,000.00
$1 1891 same	350.00	675.00
$2 1890 Gen. James D. McPherson	1,100.00	4,250.00
$2 1891 same	525.00	1,600.00
$5 1890 Gen. George H. Thomas	1,000.00	3,000.00

Two-Dollar Treasury Note, Series 1890

	F	XF
$5 1891 same	550.00	1,250.00
$10 1890 Gen. Philip H. Sheridan	1,200.00	4,500.00
$10 1891 same	900.00	2,000.00
$20 1890 John Marshall	4,000.00	8,000.00
$20 1891 same	4,750.00	8,000.00

10-Dollar Treasury Note, Series 1890

	F	XF
$50 1891 William H. Seward	—	125,000.00
$100 1890 Adm. David G. Farragut	—	180,000.00
$100 1891 same	60,000.00	140,000.00
$1,000 1890 Gen. George Meade	—	1,095,000
$1,000 1891 same, rare	—	—

NATIONAL BANK NOTES

National bank notes were a collaboration between private, nationally charted banks and the U.S. government. Individual banks could invest in U.S. bonds and, in return, receive paper money with a face value equal to their investment. The federal government designed and printed the notes. Designs were the same for each bank, but notes were imprinted with the name and charter number of the national bank receiving them. Some early notes also bear the coat of arms of the issuing bank's state.

National bank notes, titled "National Currency" on their faces, were legal tender anywhere in the United States and could be redeemed at the issuing bank or the U.S. Treasury. Notes redeemed at the Treasury were charged against the issuing bank's bond account. More than 1,300 national banks issued notes.

There were three periods during which banks could apply for a 20-year nationally issued charter: (1) 1863-1882, (2) 1882-1902, and (3) 1902-1922. Banks could issue notes under the first charter period until 1902, under the second charter period until 1922, and under the third charter period until 1929. Notes issued under each charter period have different designs.

Like all other U.S. paper money, national bank notes were reduced in size in 1929. Type 1 notes (1929-1933) list the charter number on the face twice. Type 2 notes (1933-1935) list it four times.

National bank notes were discontinued in May 1935 when the Treasury recalled many of the bonds in which the national banks had invested.

Nationals have been among the most sought-after notes in a generally active U.S. paper-money market. Not all nationals of a given type have the same value; notes of certain states and cities are more popularly collected than others. Also, some banks ordered only small quantities of notes. The values listed below are for the most common and least expensive banks issuing that type of note. Large-size nationals from Alaska, Arizona, Hawaii, Idaho, Indian Territory, Mississippi, Nevada, New Mexico, Puerto Rico, and South Dakota are worth more. The same is true for small-size nationals from Alaska, Arizona, Hawaii, Idaho, Montana, Nevada, and Wyoming.

Known Counterfeits: Examine design detail and the silk threads in the paper. Use reasonable caution.

First Charter (1863-1875)	VG	VF
$1 Allegory of Concord, no date, original series	1,200.00	1,700.00
$1 Allegory of Concord, 1875	1,200.00	1,700.00
$2 Sir Walter Raleigh, "lazy 2," no date, original series	3,600.00	5,750.00
$2 Sir Walter Raleigh, 1875	3,600.00	5,750.00

First Charter (1863-1875)	VG	VF
$5 Columbus sighting land, no date, original series	1,600.00	2,250.00
$5 Columbus sighting land, 1875	1,600.00	2,100.00
$10 Franklin flying kite, note date, original series	1,950.00	2,650.00
$10 Franklin flying kite, 1875	1,800.00	2,650.00
$20 Battle of Lexington, no date, original series	2,550.00	3,500.00
$20 Battle of Lexington, 1875	2,550.00	3,500.00
$50 Washington Crossing Delaware, no date, original series	14,000.00	16,000.00
$100 Battle of Lake Erie, no date, original series	16,000.00	20,000.00
$500, rare	—	—
$1,000, rare	—	—

Second Charter, Series of 1882 "Brown Backs" with Charter Number On Back	VG	VF
$5 James Garfield	650.00	1,250.00
$10 as first charter	1,100.00	1,650.00
$20 as first charter	1,200.00	1,850.00
$50 as first charter	5,250.00	6,000.00
$100 as first charter	6,600.00	7,500.00

Second Charter, Series of 1882 "Date Backs" with Large "1882*1908" On Back	VG	VF
$5 James Garfield	650.00	800.00
$10 as first charter	800.00	1,100.00
$20 as first charter	1,100.00	1,600.00

Second Charter, Series of 1882 "Date Backs" with Large "1882*1908" On Back	VG	VF
$50 as first charter	5,250.00	6,000.00
$100 as first charter	7,000.00	8,000.00

Second Charter, Series of 1882 "Value Backs" Large Spelled-Out Value On Back	VG	VF
$5 James Garfield	750.00	1,000.00
$10 as first charter	950.00	1,200.00
$20 as first charter	1,150.00	1,600.00
$50 as first charter, rare	—	—
$100 as second series, rare	—	—

Third Charter, Series of 1902 Red Treasury Seal On Face	VG	VF
$5 Benjamin Harrison	675.00	1,000.00
$10 William McKinley	900.00	1,200.00
$20 Hugh McCulloch	1,150.00	1,600.00
$50 John Sherman	5,500.00	6,000.00
$100 John Knox	7,000.00	9,000.00

Third Charter, Series of 1902 Blue Treasury Seal, "1902-1908" On Back	VG	VF
$5 as red seals	260.00	350.00
$10 as red seals	250.00	375.00
$20 as red seals	250.00	400.00
$50 as red seals	2,000.00	2,400.00
$100 as red seals	2,250.00	3,000.00

50-Dollar National Bank Note, Third Charter

Third Charter, Series of 1902 Blue Treasury Seal, "Plain Backs" Without Dates	VG	VF
$5 as red seals	175.00	325.00
$10 as red seals	200.00	300.00
$20 as red seals	235.00	375.00
$50 as red seals	2,000.00	3,000.00
$100 as red seals	2,750.00	3,750.00

Third Charter, Series of 1929, Brown Treasury Seal, Small-Size	VG	VF
$5 Type 1	65.00	100.00
$5 Type 2	90.00	120.00
$10 Type 1	75.00	130.00
$10 Type 2	85.00	140.00
$20 Type 1	65.00	115.00

Five-Dollar Small-Size, Type 2 National Bank Note (serial number and bank number in brown), Series 1929

Third Charter, Series of 1929, Brown Treasury Seal, Small-Size	VG	VF
$20 Type 2	75.00	130.00
$50 Type 1	425.00	675.00
$50 Type 2	475.00	750.00
$100 Type 1	560.00	675.00
$100 Type 2	675.00	750.00

50-Dollar Small-Size National Bank Note, Type 2, Series 1929

NATIONAL GOLD BANK NOTES

National gold bank notes were similar to national bank notes but were redeemable specifically in gold coin. They were issued by nationally chartered banks that were authorized by the Treasury to issue notes redeemable in gold.

They were issued from 1870 to 1875 to relieve California banks of the daily handling of massive quantities of gold coin. All but one of the banks authorized to issue the notes was located in California.

National gold bank notes were printed on golden yellow paper and bear an array of U.S. gold coins on their reverse designs. Fine engraving resulted in high-quality images.

Because other types of notes were not popular in California, national gold bank notes saw heavy use and are scarce today in collectible condition.

Known Counterfeits: Examine design detail and look for correctly colored paper, which occasionally may tone. Use reasonable caution.

	G	F
$5 Columbus sighting land	1,750.00	6,000.00
$10 Franklin flying kite	2,400.00	7,500.00
$20 Battle of Lexington	8,000.00	30,000.00
$50 Washington Crossing Delaware, rare	—	—
$100 Battle of Lake Erie, rare	—	—

UNITED STATES NOTES

Most of these notes are titled "United States Note" at the top or bottom of their faces, but some earlier ones are titled "Treasury Note." The first United States notes omit both, but all were authorized under the same legislation. They were issued for over a century (1862-1966) and thus are the longest-running type of U.S. paper money.

The series contains many classic designs. The most popular is the $10 with a bison on its face.

Like other currency, United States Notes were reduced in size with the Series 1928, printed in 1929. Small-size United States notes occasionally are still found in circulation today and are characterized by a red Treasury seal. They generally are not collected in worn condition.

This series includes popular "star notes," which have part of the serial number replaced by a star. They were printed to replace notes accidentally destroyed in manufacturing. These were introduced on $20 notes in 1880 and eventually descended to $1 notes by 1917. They usually are worth more than regularly numbered notes.

Known Counterfeits: Examine design detail and the silk threads in the paper. Use reasonable caution. In addition to counterfeits made to deceive collectors, early circulation counterfeits of the 1863 $50, 1869 $50, and 1863 $100 exist.

Two-Dollar Large-Size United States Note, Series 1875

Large Size	F	VF
$1 1862 Salmon P. Chase, red seal	550.00	1,000.00
$1 1869 George Washington	500.00	1,500.00
$1 1880 George Washington	200.00	400.00
$1 1923 George Washington	135.00	240.00
$2 1862 Alexander Hamilton	800.00	2,000.00
$2 1869 Jefferson, Capitol	800.00	2,000.00

Five-Dollar Large-Size United States Note, Series 1869

Large Size	F	VF
$2 1880 Jefferson, Capitol	250.00	600.00
$5 1862 Statue of Columbia, Alexander Hamilton	525.00	1,450.00
$5 1863 same, different obligation on back	575.00	1,150.00
$5 1869 Andrew Jackson, pioneer family	600.00	1,200.00
$5 1875 same, red seal	600.00	1,325.00
$5 1880 same, brown seal	440.00	850.00

10-Dollar Large-Size United States Note, Series 1862

Large Size	F	VF
$10 1862 Lincoln, allegory of art	1,400.00	2,500.00
$10 1863 same, different obligation on back	1,250.00	3,900.00
$10 1869 Daniel Webster, Pocahontas	700.00	1,500.00
$10 1880 Daniel Webster, Pocahontas	700.00	1,750.00
$10 1880 same, brown seal	565.00	1,100.00
$10 1901 bison	900.00	2,900.00

10-Dollar Large-Size United States Note, Series 1901

Large Size	F	VF
$10 1923 Andrew Jackson	1,200.00	3,500.00
$20 1862 Liberty with sword and shield	2,250.00	6,750.00
$20 1863 same, different obligation on back	2,250.00	6,750.00
$20 1869 Alexander Hamilton, Victory	2,100.00	5,000.00
$20 1878 same, no inscription at center on back	1,100.00	2,500.00
$20 1880 same, brown seal	2,000.00	4,750.00

Large Size	F	VF
$50 1862 Alexander Hamilton	23,000.00	58,000.00
$50 1863 same, different obligation on back	12,500.00	57,500.00
$50 1869 Peace, Henry Clay	15,000.00	65,000.00
$50 1874 Benjamin Franklin, Columbia	15,000.00	35,000.00
$50 1880 same, brown seal	7,000.00	15,750.00
$100 1862 eagle	30,000.00	50,000.00
$100 1863 same, different obligation on back, rare	—	—
$100 1869 Lincoln, allegory of Architecture	12,500.00	30,000.00
$100 1880 same, inscription at left on back	10,000.00	27,500.00
$100 1880 same, brown seal	9,000.00	30,000.00
$500 1862 Albert Gallatin, rare	—	—
$500 1863 same, different obligation on back, rare	—	—
$500 1869 John Quincy Adams, rare	—	—
$500 1880 Gen. Joseph Mansfield, rare	—	—
$500 1880 same, brown seal, rare	—	—
$1,000 1862 Robert Morris, rare	—	—
$1,000 1863 same, different obligation on back, rare	—	—
$1,000 1869 Columbus, DeWitt Clinton, rare	—	—
$1,000 1880 same, inscription at left, rare	—	—
$1,000 1880 same, brown seal, rare	—	—

SMALL-SIZE U.S. NOTES, RED SEAL

Denom.	Issue	Front	Back
$1	1928	Washington	ONE
$2	1928-63A	Jefferson	Monticello
$5	1928-63	Lincoln	Lincoln Memorial
$100	1966-66A	Franklin	Indep. Hall

Small Size	F	XF
$1 1928	125.00	150.00
$2 1928	10.00	20.00
$2 1928A	40.00	100.00
$2 1928B	80.00	300.00
$2 1928C	20.00	30.00
$2 1928D	10.00	35.00
$2 1928E	15.00	25.00
$2 1928F	15.00	25.00
$2 1928G	7.50	10.00
$5 1928	10.00	20.00
$5 1928A	15.00	50.00
$5 1928B	15.00	30.00
$5 1928C	12.50	25.00

One-Dollar Small-Size United States Note, Red Seal, Series 1928

Small Size	F	XF
$5 1928D	35.00	75.00
$5 1928E	10.00	25.00
$5 1928F	10.00	25.00
$5 1953	10.00	15.00
$5 1953A	7.50	15.00

Five-Dollar Small-Size United States Note, Red Seal, Series 1928

Small Size	F	XF
$5 1953B	7.50	15.00
$5 1953C	7.50	25.00
$5 1963	7.50	15.00
$100 1966	125.00	210.00
$100 1966A	225.00	400.00

Small Size	CU
$2 1953	10.00
$2 1953A	10.00
$2 1953B	10.00
$2 1953C	10.00
$2 1963	8.00
$2 1963A	10.00

GOLD CERTIFICATES

As the title on these notes implies, gold certificates were backed by reserves of gold coin and payable to the bearer in that coin. The first gold certificates were issued from 1865 to 1875 but were used only for transactions between banks. Notes of this period not listed here are not known to have survived. The issue of 1882 was the first for general circulation. Only $5,000 and $10,000 notes were issued in 1888-1889 and did not circulate widely.

Regular issues were again placed in circulation from 1905 to 1907. This series includes a $20 note so beautifully colored with black, red, and gold ink on white, gold-tinted paper that collectors have nicknamed it "Technicolor." Gold certificates of Series 1913-1928 are the most common.

Gold certificates were reduced in size beginning with Series 1928. The small-size notes have a gold Treasury seal.

The final gold certificates, of 1934, were again issued just for bank transactions. The government recalled these notes from general circulation in 1933 when it withdrew gold coinage. Today, they are legal to own but are scarce because of the recall.

Known Counterfeits: Examine design detail on 1882 and later notes and the silk threads in the paper on all notes. Use reasonable caution.

First Issue, 1863	F	XF
$20 eagle on shield	—	500,000.00
$100 eagle on shield, rare	—	—

Second Issue, 1870-71		
No notes known to have survived.		

Third Issue, 1875		
$100 Thomas H. Benton, rare	—	—

Fourth Issue, Series of 1882	F	XF
$20 James Garfield	8,500.00	14,750.00
$50 Silas Wright	975.00	5,000.00
$100 Thomas Benton	1,150.00	8,000.00
$500 Abraham Lincoln	7,000.00	18,750.00
$1,000 Alexander Hamilton	97,750.00	—
$5,000 James Madison, rare	—	—
$10,000 Andrew Jackson, rare	—	—

Fifth Issue, Series of 1888	F	XF
$5,000 James Madison, rare	—	—
$10,000 Andrew Jackson, rare	—	—

Sixth Issue, Series of 1900	F	XF
$10,000 Jackson	1,750.00	3,750.00

Seventh Issue, Series of 1905-1907	F	XF
$10 Michael Hillegas	250.00	575.00
$20 1905 George Washington, "Technicolor"	1,250.00	6,900.00
$20 1906 George Washington	300.00	600.00

Eighth Issue, Series of 1907	F	XF
$1,000 Alexander Hamilton	—	37,500.00

Ninth Issue, Series of 1913	F	XF
$50 Ulysses S. Grant	600.00	2,500.00

Tenth Issue, Series of 1922	F	XF
$10 Michael Hillegas	250.00	600.00
$20 Washington	300.00	575.00
$50 Ulysses S. Grant	600.00	2,500.00
$100 Thomas Benton	1,000.00	4,000.00
$500 Abraham Lincoln, rare	—	—
$1,000 Alexander Hamilton, rare	—	—

Small Size, Series of 1928	F	XF
$10 Alexander Hamilton	90.00	250.00

10-Dollar Small-Size Gold Certificate, Series 1928

Small Size, Series of 1928	F	XF
$20 Andrew Jackson	100.00	250.00
$50 Ulysses S. Grant	250.00	1,250.00
$100 Benjamin Franklin	300.00	1,250.00
$500 William McKinley	3,450.00	10,000.00
$1,000 Grover Cleveland	2,750.00	12,500.00
$5,000 James Madison, unique	—	—

SILVER CERTIFICATES

On Feb. 28, 1878, the same day Congress authorized the striking of millions of silver dollars, it also passed legislation authorizing silver certificates. The notes represented actual silver dollars held by the U.S. Treasury. The legislation passed in response to lobbying by silver-mining interests.

Some of the most famous and beautiful bank notes issued by the United States are silver certificates. These include the "educational" $1, $2, and $5 notes of 1896; the "One Papa" $5; and the "porthole" $5. "One Papa" is a misnomer. The note actually depicts Chief Running Antelope of the Uncpapa Sioux, but because the name was unfamiliar to early collectors, it was mispronounced "Chief One Papa."

Like other U.S. paper money, silver certificates were reduced in size with Series 1928, in 1929.

During World War II, there was fear that supplies of U.S. currency would fall into enemy hands if certain territories were lost. In response, notes distributed in these territories were given distinguishing features that permitted their identification and repudiation if captured. Silver certificates issued to troops in North Africa were printed with a yellow Treasury seal instead of a blue one. Notes distributed in Hawaii featured the word "Hawaii" overprinted in large letters on the back.

The motto "In God We Trust" was added to the $1 note for Series 1935G and 1935H, and all 1957 series. Silver certificates continued until Series 1957B, in 1963. Small-size silver certificates are occasionally found in circulation today and are easily recognized by their blue Treasury seal. When worn, these notes are generally not collectible but do have some novelty value. They have not been redeemable for silver dollars since 1968.

This series includes popular "star notes," which have part of the serial number replaced by a star. They were printed to replace notes accidentally destroyed in the manufacturing process. Star notes were introduced in 1899. They often, but not always, are worth somewhat more than regularly numbered pieces.

Known Counterfeits: Examine design detail and the silk threads in the paper. Use reasonable caution. Circulating counterfeits exist for this series and are slightly less dangerous than those made to deceive the collector market.

One-Dollar Large-Size Silver Certificate, Series 1896

Large Size	F	XF
$1 1886 Martha Washington	300.00	875.00
$1 1891 Martha Washington	400.00	850.00
$1 1896 History instructing youth	400.00	1,500.00
$1 1899 eagle	150.00	350.00
$1 1923 George Washington	50.00	90.00

Two-Dollar Large-Size Silver Certificate, Series 1896

Large Size	F	XF
$2 1886 Gen. Winfield Scott Hancock	675.00	1,750.00
$2 1891 William Windom	625.00	2,000.00
$2 1896 Science presenting steam and electricity to Commerce and Industry	850.00	3,000.00
$2 1899 George Washington, Mechanics and Agriculture	325.00	675.00

Five-Dollar Large-Size Silver Certificate, Series 1899

Large Size	F	XF
$5 1886 Ulysses S. Grant	1,000.00	4,500.00
$5 1891 Ulysses S. Grant	750.00	2,000.00
$5 1896 winged Electricity lighting the World	1,200.00	4,500.00
$5 1899 Chief "One Papa"	650.00	1,700.00
$5 1923 Abraham Lincoln	900.00	2,750.00
$10 1880 Robert Morris	1,700.00	5,250.00

10-Dollar Large-Size Silver Certificate, 1891 Series

Large Size	F	XF
$10 1886 Thomas Hendricks	1,250.00	4,500.00
$10 1891 Thomas Hendricks	750.00	1,500.00
$20 1878 Capt. Stephen Decatur	5,000.00	18,000.00
$20 1886 Daniel Manning	5,000.00	20,000.00
$20 1891 Daniel Manning	1,500.00	3,750.00
$50 1878 Edward Everett	37,000.00	—

Large Size	F	XF
$50 1891 Edward Everett	4,500.00	8,500.00
$100 1880 James Monroe	16,000.00	45,000.00
$100 1891 James Monroe	8,000.00	30,000.00
$500 1880 Sen. Charles Sumner	—	420,000.00
$1,000 1880 William Marcy	—	580,000.00
$1,000 1891 Columbia, Marcy, rare	—	—

SMALL-SIZE SILVER CERTIFICATES, BLUE SEAL

Denom.	Issue	Front	Back
$1	1928-28E	Washington	ONE
$1	1934-57B	Washington	Great Seal
$5	1934-53C	Lincoln	Lincoln Memorial
$10	1933-53B	Hamilton	Treasury

One-Dollar Small-Size Silver Certificate, Blue Seal, Series 1928

Small Size, Blue Seal	VF	CU
$1 1928	30.00	40.00
$1 1928A	20.00	40.00
$1 1928B	25.00	40.00
$1 1928C	350.00	500.00
$1 1928D	100.00	300.00
$1 1928E	600.00	1,500.00

Small Size, Blue Seal	VF	CU
$1 1934	30.00	60.00
$1 1935	10.00	20.00
$1 1935A	2.75	10.00
$1 1935A "Hawaii"	40.00	100.00
$1 1935A, yellow seal	50.00	100.00
$1 1935A, red R	75.00	300.00
$1 1935A, red S	75.00	300.00
$1 1935B	3.00	12.00
$1 1935C	3.00	10.00
$1 1935D	4.00	9.00
$1 1935E	3.00	6.00
$1 1935F	2.50	6.00
$1 1935G	4.00	8.00
$1 1935G, with motto	5.00	60.00
$1 1935H	3.00	10.00
$1 1957	2.50	5.00
$1 1957A	2.50	6.50
$1 1957B	2.50	6.50
$5 1934	8.00	34.00
$5 1934A	8.00	20.00
$5 1934A, yellow seal	80.00	200.00
$5 1934B	15.00	45.00

Five-Dollar Small-Size Silver Certificate, Special Yellow Seal, Series 1934A

Small Size, Blue Seal	VF	CU
$5 1934C	8.00	25.00
$5 1934D	8.00	20.00
$5 1953	12.50	40.00
$5 1953A	10.00	40.00
$5 1953B	8.00	16.00

Five-Dollar Small-Size Silver Certificate, Blue Seal, Series 1934B

Small Size, Blue Seal	F	XF
$10 1933	6,000.00	12,500.00
$10 1933A, rare	—	—
$10 1934	50.00	150.00
$10 1934A	40.00	150.00
$10 1934, yellow seal	6,000.00	20,000.00

10-Dollar Small-Size Silver Certificate, Blue Seal, Series 1933

Small Size, Blue Seal	F	XF
$10 1934A, yellow seal	60.00	300.00
$10 1934B	500.00	2,250.00
$10 1934C	40.00	200.00
$10 1934D	40.00	150.00
$10 1953	50.00	250.00

10-Dollar Small-Size Silver Certificate,
Special Yellow Seal, Series 1934A

Small Size, Blue Seal	F	XF
$10 1953A	100.00	400.00
$10 1953B	25.00	200.00

FEDERAL RESERVE NOTES

The Federal Reserve System was created in 1913. It consists of 12 Federal Reserve banks governed in part by the U.S. government through the Federal Reserve Board, whose members are appointed by the president and confirmed by the Senate. Each of the Federal Reserve banks is composed of various member banks.

The paper money we use today in the United States is issued by the Federal Reserve banks. Originally Federal Reserve notes could be redeemed for gold. That changed in 1934.

Like all other U.S. paper money, Federal Reserve notes were reduced in size with Series 1928, in 1929.

Since 1993, new anti-counterfeiting innovations have been added to the notes. Micro printing was incorporated in the design and around the frame of the portrait. Also, a transparent strip bearing the value and "USA" was embedded in the paper. It can be seen only when the note is held up to a light and cannot be photocopied.

These improvements were precursors to the first major overhaul of U.S. paper money since the 1920s. Beginning with the $100 bill in 1996, more changes were made, including larger portraits to show more detail and more white space on the reverse so watermarks could be added to the paper. A watermark is an image pressed against the paper while the newly printed note is drying. Like the transparent printed strip, it can be seen only when the note is held up to a light.

Among the most ingenious high-tech safeguards on the new notes is color-shifting ink, which alters its color depending on the angle of the light hitting it. The green Treasury seal has been retained, but the old letter seal indicating the Federal Reserve bank of distribution was replaced by the Federal Reserve System seal. These innovations were added to the $20 and $50 notes with Series 1996 and the $5 and $10 notes with Series 1999. The $1 note was not scheduled to change.

In 2004, additional steps were taken to prevent counterfeiting. The $10, $20, and $50 notes received multicolored background designs. New $5 notes with the changes were released in March 2008. The changes are also slated for the $100 note.

Federal Reserve notes are produced at the Bureau of Engraving and Printing's main facility in Washington, D.C., and at its Western Currency Facility in Fort Worth, Texas. Notes produced at Fort Worth have a small "FW" mark in the lower right corner of the face.

Most Federal Reserve notes produced since the 1930s are collected only in high grade. Dealers may be unwilling to buy even scarce pieces if they are not crisp uncirculated. Star notes, which have a star instead of one of the numerals in their serial numbers, are popularly collected in this series but, again, must be crisp to be desirable. Recent issues command no premium; they are sold at face value plus a handling fee to cover the dealer's labor.

Known Counterfeits: Examine design detail and the silk threads in the paper. Use reasonable caution. Circulating counterfeits exist, particularly of the $20 and to a lesser extent the $10. Most are imperfect and can be easily detected on close examination. The $100 is the most counterfeited note outside the United States.

10-Dollar Large-Size Federal
Reserve Note, Red Seal, Series 1914

*Five-Dollar Large-Size Federal
Reserve Note, Blue Seal, Series 1914*

Red Seal, Series of 1914	F	XF
$5 Abraham Lincoln	425.00	850.00
$10 Andrew Jackson	750.00	1,500.00
$20 Grover Cleveland	725.00	4,400.00
$50 Ulysses S. Grant	2,750.00	4,500.00
$100 Benjamin Franklin	1,750.00	3,750.00

*10-Dollar Large-Size Federal
Reserve Note, Blue Seal, Series 1914*

Blue Seal, Series of 1914	F	XF
$5 Abraham Lincoln	85.00	175.00
$10 Andrew Jackson	100.00	225.00
$20 Grover Cleveland	225.00	400.00
$50 Ulysses S. Grant	500.00	1,100.00
$100 Benjamin Franklin	650.00	1,000.00

*1,000-Dollar Large-Size Federal
Reserve Note, Blue Seal, Series 1918*

Blue Seal, Series of 1918	F	XF
$500 John Marshall	16,500.00	—
$1,000 Alexander Hamilton	14,000.00	—
$5,000 James Madison, rare	—	—
$10,000 Salmon P. Chase, rare	—	—

SMALL-SIZE NOTES, GREEN SEAL

Denom.	Issue	Front	Back
$1	1963	Washington	Great Seal
$2	1976	Jefferson	Signing Declaration
$5	1928	Lincoln	Lincoln Memorial
$10	1928	Hamilton	Treasury Building
$20	1928	Jackson	White House
$50	1928	Grant	Capitol
$100	1928	Franklin	Independence Hall
$500	1928-34A	McKinley	500
$1,000	1928-34A	Cleveland	inscription
$5,000	1928-34B	Madison	5,000
$10,000	1928-34B	Chase	10,000

One-Dollar Small-Size Federal
Reserve Note, Green Seal, Series 1963

One Dollar	XF	CU
1963	2.00	3.00
1963A	2.00	3.00
1963B	3.00	3.50
1969	1.50	2.50
1969A	1.50	2.50

One Dollar	XF	CU
1969B	1.50	2.50
1969C	2.00	2.50
1969D	2.00	2.50
1974	2.00	3.00
1977	2.00	3.00
1977A	2.00	3.00
1981	—	2.00
1981A	1.50	3.00
1985	—	2.00
1988	—	3.00
1988A, DC	—	2.00
1988A, FW	—	2.00
1988A, web press	10.00	45.00
1993, DC	—	2.00
1993, FW	1.50	4.00
1993, web press	5.00	20.00
1995, DC	—	3.00
1995, FW	—	5.00
1995, web press	5.00	17.00
1999, DC	—	2.00
1999, FW	—	2.00
2001, DC		2.00
2001, FW	—	2.00

One-Dollar Small-Size Federal Reserve Note, Green Seal, Series 2001DC

One Dollar	XF	CU
2003, DC	—	2.00
2003, FW	—	2.00

Two Dollars	XF	CU
1976	—	4.00
1995	—	4.00

Five-Dollar Small-Size Federal
Reserve Note, Green Seal, Series 1928A

Two Dollars	XF	CU
2003, DC	—	2.00
2003A, FW	—	35.00

Five Dollars	XF	CU
1928	85.00	250.00
1928A	50.00	100.00

*Five-Dollar Small-Size Federal
Reserve Note, Green Seal, Series 1934*

Five Dollars	XF	CU
1928B	25.00	50.00
1928C	2,500.00	3,500.00
1928D	3,500.00	5,000.00
1934	20.00	45.00
1934A	20.00	30.00
1934, "Hawaii"	200.00	450.00

Five-Dollar Small-Size Federal
Reserve Note, Green Seal, Series 1950A

Five Dollars	XF	CU
1934A, "Hawaii"	200.00	450.00
1934B	20.00	40.00
1934C	20.00	50.00
1934D	25.00	50.00
1950	12.00	45.00
1950A	—	20.00

*Five-Dollar Small-Size Federal
Reserve Note, Green Seal, Series 1969*

Five Dollars	XF	CU
1950B	—	25.00
1950C	—	15.00
1950D	—	20.00
1950E	—	25.00
1963	12.50	15.00

Five Dollars	XF	CU
1963A	7.00	12.00
1969	7.00	10.00
1969A	8.00	12.00
1969B	30.00	35.00
1969C	7.00	12.00
1974	7.00	10.00
1977	7.00	15.00
1977A	10.00	35.00
1981	—	25.00
1981A	—	30.00
1985	—	15.00
1988	—	10.00
1988A	—	10.00
1993	—	10.00
1995	—	10.00
1999, large portrait	—	10.00
2001	—	10.00
2003	—	10.00

10-Dollar Small-Size Federal
Reserve Note, Green Seal, Series 1928

Ten Dollars	XF	CU
1928	60.00	250.00
1928A	60.00	400.00
1928B	30.00	65.00
1928C	60.00	350.00
1934	18.00	45.00

10-Dollar Small-Size Federal
Reserve Note, Green Seal, Series 1934

Ten Dollars	XF	CU
1934A	15.00	30.00
1934A, "HAWAII"	400.00	750.00
1934B	25.00	75.00
1934C	15.00	30.00
1934D	15.00	35.00

10-Dollar Small-Size Federal
Reserve Note, Green Seal, Series 1950A

Ten Dollars	XF	CU
1950	20.00	65.00
1950A	30.00	35.00
1950B	20.00	35.00
1950C	25.00	35.00
1950D	—	35.00
1950E	55.00	80.00

10-Dollar Small-Size Federal
Reserve Note, Green Seal, Series 1969

Ten Dollars	XF	CU
1963	—	35.00
1963A	20.00	25.00
1969	—	25.00
1969A	—	25.00
1969B	—	100.00
1969C	—	30.00

10-Dollar Small-Size Federal
Reserve Note, Green Seal, Series 1977

Ten Dollars	XF	CU
1974	—	25.00
1977	—	30.00
1977A	—	25.00
1981	—	35.00
1981A	—	35.00
1985	—	25.00

10-Dollar Small-Size Federal
Reserve Note, Green Seal, Series 2003

Ten Dollars	XF	CU
1988A	—	25.00
1990	—	15.00
1993	—	15.00
1995	—	20.00
1999, large portrait	—	15.00
2001	—	20.00
2003	—	15.00

*20-Dollar Small-Size Federal
Reserve Note, Green Seal, Series 1928*

Twenty Dollars	XF	CU
1928	100.00	175.00
1928A	150.00	300.00
1928B	50.00	100.00
1928C	800.00	2,500.00
1934	40.00	45.00
1934A	40.00	60.00

20-Dollar Small-Size Federal
Reserve Note, Green Seal, Series 1934

Twenty Dollars	XF	CU
1934, "Hawaii"	500.00	2,000.00
1934A, "Hawaii"	200.00	700.00
1934B	35.00	75.00
1934C	40.00	75.00
1934D	—	45.00
1950	—	60.00

20-Dollar Small-Size Federal
Reserve Note, Green Seal, Series 1950D

Twenty Dollars	XF	CU
1950A	—	60.00
1950B	—	45.00
1950C	—	60.00
1950D	—	60.00
1950E	65.00	100.00
1963	—	60.00

20-Dollar Small-Size Federal
Reserve Note, Green Seal, Series 1974

Twenty Dollars	XF	CU
1963A	—	45.00
1969	30.00	45.00
1969A	—	55.00
1969B	100.00	150.00
1969C	—	45.00
1974	—	45.00

*50-Dollar Small-Size Federal
Reserve Note, Green Seal, Series 1928*

Twenty Dollars	XF	CU
1977	—	45.00
1981	—	60.00
1981A	—	45.00
1985	—	40.00
1988A	—	45.00
1990	—	30.00
1993	—	30.00
1995	—	30.00
1996, large portrait	—	30.00
1999	—	30.00
2001, DC	—	30.00
2001, FW	—	30.00
2004, colorized background	—	30.00
2004A, colorized background	—	30.00

Fifty Dollars	XF	CU
1928	150.00	800.00
1928A	90.00	300.00
1934	60.00	225.00
1934A	125.00	350.00
1934B	125.00	300.00
1934C	125.00	250.00
1934D	200.00	250.00

*50-Dollar Small-Size Federal
Reserve Note, Green Seal, Series 1950*

Fifty Dollars	XF	CU
1950	—	200.00
1950A	—	200.00
1950B	—	150.00
1950C	—	150.00
1950D	—	150.00

50-Dollar Small-Size Federal
Reserve Note, Green Seal, Series 1969A

Fifty Dollars	XF	CU
1950E	375.00	750.00
1963A	—	200.00
1969	—	150.00
1969A	—	150.00
1969B	600.00	800.00

Fifty Dollars	XF	CU
1969C	—	100.00
1974	—	150.00
1977	—	125.00
1981	—	125.00
1981A	—	150.00
1985	—	75.00
1988	—	100.00
1990	—	75.00
1993	—	85.00
1996, large portrait	—	55.00
2001	—	60.00
2004, colorized background	—	60.00

*100-Dollar Small-Size Federal
Reserve Note, Green Seal, Series 1928A*

One Hundred Dollars	XF	CU
1928	250.00	600.00
1928A	200.00	275.00
1934	175.00	250.00
1934A	225.00	350.00
1934B	450.00	700.00

100-Dollar Small-Size Federal
Reserve Note, Green Seal, Series 1934B

One Hundred Dollars	XF	CU
1934C	175.00	400.00
1934D	350.00	450.00
1950	200.00	450.00
1950A	—	200.00
1950B	—	250.00

100-Dollar Small-Size Federal
Reserve Note, Green Seal, Series 1963A

One Hundred Dollars	XF	CU
1950C	—	250.00
1950D	—	250.00
1950E	375.00	750.00
1963A	—	200.00
1969	125.00	175.00

One Hundred Dollars	XF	CU
1969A	—	175.00
1969C	—	175.00
1974	—	150.00
1977	—	175.00
1981	—	200.00
1981A	—	200.00
1985	—	150.00
1988	—	150.00
1990	—	125.00
1993	—	120.00
1996, large portrait	—	120.00
1999	—	125.00
2001	—	115.00
2003	—	115.00
2003A	—	115.00

Five Hundred Dollars	XF	CU
1928	1,600.00	3,000.00
1934	850.00	1,000.00
1934A	1,250.00	1,750.00
1934B, specimens only	—	—
1934C, specimens only	—	—

One Thousand Dollars	XF	CU
1928	2,500.00	4,000.00
1934	2,000.00	3,000.00
1934A	2,000.00	2,500.00
1934C, specimens only	—	—

Five Thousand Dollars	XF	CU
1928	40,000.00	90,000.00
1934	35,000.00	50,000.00
1934A	—	—
1934B	—	—

Ten Thousand Dollars	XF	CU
1928	90,000.00	100,000.00
1934	60,000.00	80,000.00
1934A, specimens only	—	—
1934B, none privately owned	—	—

FEDERAL RESERVE BANK NOTES

Federal Reserve bank notes were another type of national currency but were issued by the 12 Federal Reserve banks rather than nationally chartered private banks. They were legal tender but not a government obligation; the obligation to redeem was with the Federal Reserve banks, not the U.S. Treasury.

Large-size notes have a blue Treasury seal on them. Small-size Federal Reserve bank notes were actually emergency currency printed on notes originally intended to become regular Series 1929 national currency. They were issued in 1933 and have a brown Treasury seal.

The name of the issuing Federal Reserve bank is printed on the note in the same location as the issuing bank on a national bank note.

Star notes are scarce and command a significant premium.

Known Counterfeits: Examine design detail and the silk threads in the paper. Use reasonable caution.

Large Size	F	XF
$1 1918 George Washington	125.00	250.00
$2 1918 Thomas Jefferson	700.00	850.00
$5 1915 Abraham Lincoln	250.00	500.00
$5 1918 same	400.00	650.00

One-Dollar Large-Size Federal
Reserve Bank Note, Series 1918

Large Size	F	XF
$10 1915 Andrew Jackson	1,300.00	2,750.00
$10 1918 same	1,250.00	2,750.00
$20 1915 Grover Cleveland	2,000.00	3,500.00
$20 1918 same	2,275.00	3,750.00
$50 1918 Ulysses S. Grant	5,000.00	10,000.00

Five-Dollar Small-Size Federal
Reserve Bank Note, Brown Seal, Series 1929

Small Size, Brown Seal	XF	CU
$5 Boston	60.00	100.00
$5 New York	50.00	100.00
$5 Philadelphia	75.00	100.00
$5 Cleveland	50.00	100.00
$5 Atlanta	75.00	125.00

10-Dollar Small-Size Federal Reserve
Bank Note, Brown Seal, Series 1929

Small Size, Brown Seal	XF	CU
$5 Chicago	50.00	100.00
$5 St. Louis	1,500.00	2,000.00
$5 Minneapolis	225.00	650.00
$5 Kansas City	225.00	650.00
$5 Dallas	75.00	300.00

Small Size, Brown Seal	XF	CU
$5 San Francisco	4,000.00	10,000.00
$10 Boston	75.00	275.00
$10 New York	60.00	200.00
$10 Philadelphia	65.00	250.00
$10 Cleveland	60.00	150.00
$10 Richmond	100.00	275.00
$10 Atlanta	75.00	200.00
$10 Chicago	70.00	200.00
$10 St. Louis	60.00	120.00
$10 Minneapolis	75.00	250.00
$10 Kansas City	50.00	200.00
$10 Dallas	750.00	1,200.00
$10 San Francisco	500.00	1,000.00
$20 Boston	75.00	250.00
$20 New York	50.00	200.00
$20 Philadelphia	100.00	250.00
$20 Cleveland	70.00	230.00
$20 Richmond	175.00	400.00
$20 Atlanta	150.00	650.00
$20 Chicago	60.00	150.00
$20 St. Louis	100.00	150.00
$20 Minneapolis	100.00	250.00
$20 Kansas City	150.00	350.00

20-Dollar Small-Size Federal
Reserve Bank Note, Brown Seal, Series 1929

Small Size, Brown Seal	XF	CU
$20 Dallas	500.00	2,500.00
$20 San Francisco	200.00	300.00
$50 New York	150.00	225.00
$50 Cleveland	115.00	300.00
$50 Chicago	100.00	200.00

100-Dollar Small-Size Federal
Reserve Bank Note, Brown Seal, Series 1929

Small Size, Brown Seal	XF	CU
$50 Minneapolis	250.00	500.00
$50 Kansas City	160.00	375.00
$50 Dallas	750.00	5,000.00
$50 San Francisco	300.00	400.00
$100 New York	165.00	400.00

Small Size, Brown Seal	XF	CU
$100 Cleveland	175.00	275.00
$100 Richmond	300.00	700.00
$100 Chicago	225.00	450.00
$100 Minneapolis	300.00	600.00
$100 Kansas City	210.00	350.00
$100 Dallas	1,500.00	2,300.00

INDEX

COINS BY DENOMINATION

PAPER MONEY BY ISSUE

ALPHABETICAL LISTING